50 LESSONS
I Learned From
THE WORLD'S #1
GOAL ACHIEVER

Vic Johnson

Published by:

Laurenzana Press

PO Box 1220

Melrose, FL 32666 USA

www.LaurenzanaPress.com

****

© Copyright 2014 Laurenzana Press. All rights reserved. No part of this book may be reproduced in any form or by any means without the prior written permission of the Publisher.
ISBN-13: 978-1-937918-79-8

FREE
SMART Goals Worksheet and step-by-step video
available for immediate download.
www.Get-Smart-Goals.com

TABLE OF CONTENTS

INTRODUCTION: THE LIFE AND LESSONS OF JOHN GODDARD ix

LESSON 1: DEFINING BLISS 1
- Action: Answer six important questions, and then create a life list that excites you.

LESSON 2: THINK OUTSIDE THE BOX 5
- What Would John Goddard Do?
- Action: Identify your goal, and take a radical step to achieve it.

LESSON 3: DON'T JUST DREAM IT – BE IT! 8
- Action: Make an identity dream board or mind map. Then adapt to your new persona.

LESSON 4: MAKE FRIENDS WHEREVER YOU GO 11
- Action: Initiate with one positive, inspiring person; and pull away from one negative, sabotaging person.

LESSON 5: MAKE A DIFFERENCE 14
- Action: Give generously of your time or resources to someone who has the same goals.

LESSON 6: IMAGINE IT'S ALREADY DONE 16
- Action: Spend time fantasizing about your success.

LESSON 7: MAKE EVERY MINUTE COUNT 18
- Stay Focused on Your Goal.
- Action: Identify and eliminate two hours of wasted time.

LESSON 8: LEARN FROM YOUR DISASTERS 21
- Have Realistic Perspectives.
- Action: Make a list of possible disasters that could stop you from meeting your goals.

LESSON 9: DISASTERS CAN BE BLESSINGS 24
- Action: Every night write down two blessings that happen each day, and focus on how the good of those blessings will carry you toward your goals.

LESSON 10: FOCUS ON THE GOOD 26
- Action: Post sticky notes where you can frequently see them documenting good experiences you've had.

LESSON 11: CREATE VISUALIZATION TOOLS 28
- Action: Create an inspirational image, put it where you can see it often.

LESSON 12: FALL IN LOVE WITH YOUR DREAMS 31
- Defining Your Passion
- Getting On the Right Path
- Action: Surround yourself with visual aids that inspire you to pursue your goal.

LESSON 13: NEVER FEAR FAILURE 34
- All You Need is One...
- Action: Find a failure-proof mentor.

LESSON 14: FACE YOUR FEARS 37
- Action: Take action to face your fears.

LESSON 15: IGNORE THE NAYSAYERS 41
- Action: Ask a friend or accountability partner to be brutally honest about what they see is holding you back.

LESSON 16: TUNE OUT OTHER PEOPLE'S FEARS 44
- Action: Walk away from negative relationships that bring you down.

LESSON 17: PERSISTENCE PAYS OFF 46
- Action: Devise a reward plan for yourself.

LESSON 18: CREATE A WIN-WIN SITUATION 49
- Action: Look for ways to contribute to something that will provide valuable exposure, training, experience or inspiration.

LESSON 19: BEGIN WITH A PLAN 51
- Action: Make an action plan that requires you to think through the details of accomplishing your goal.

LESSON 20: STAY AWAY FROM THE HERD 53
- Action: Initiate contact with someone who inspires you and who you think is out of your league.

LESSON 21: ELIMINATE LIMITING SELF-TALK 56
- Action: Write down one thing you did right, and read it out loud before you go to bed and before you start the next day.

LESSON 22: PROVE YOURSELF 59
- Action: Set a milestone goal that will be difficult to meet, and then crush that goal!

LESSON 23: AVOID PROCRASTINATION 62
- Action: Create a mantra and a totem.

LESSON 24: AVOID WHERE ANGELS FEAR TO TREAD 64
- Action: Brainstorm new and improved routes to success.

LESSON 25: HAVE A "SOUL GOAL" 67
- Action: Focus only on actions that feed your soul. Take a break from activities that feel like work or you feel pressured to perform. Let your soul breathe.

LESSON 26: COMMIT TO NATURE 70
- Action: Get out into nature every day.

LESSON 27: WRITE IT DOWN 73
- Action: Write a contract to yourself promising you'll focus on your goals.

LESSON 28: GIVE YOUR GOALS A DEADLINE 75
- Action: Create a milestone plan for your goals.

LESSON 29: GIVE YOUR GOALS A BUDGET 77
- Action: Establish a time and/or money budget.

LESSON 30: WHAT YOU RESIST PERSISTS 79
- Action: Write a three to five-word mantra.

LESSON 31: MENTALLY REHEARSE THE OUTCOME 82
- Action: Prepare a narration of how you see the event.

LESSON 32: PROGRAM YOUR SUBCONSCIOUS 84
- Action: Listen to your five-minute narration as you go to sleep each night.

LESSON 33: DO YOUR HOMEWORK 86
- Action: Devote a set amount of time for research and for asking questions.

LESSON 34: GET OVER YOURSELF 89
- Action: Carve out two extra hours you'll devote to pursuing your goal.

LESSON 35: SEE THE BIG PICTURE 91
- Action: Make a storyboard of your big picture.

LESSON 36: TAKE CARE OF YOUR BODY 94
- Action: Choose a healthy habit to pursue (or an unhealthy habit to quit) that will affect your overall health.

LESSON 37: COUNT YOUR BLESSINGS 97
- Action: Think about something you're grateful for every day, and then verbalize your gratitude.

LESSON 38: STAY SAFE BUT CURIOUS 100
- Action: Meet with a friend, mentor or partner to discuss your life list in detail.

LESSON 39: FEED YOUR MIND 103
- Action: Find a book or eBook about one of your goals. Read it or listen to it on audiobook.

LESSON 40: LEARN FROM ROLE MODELS 105
- Action: Go online, read forums, go to a seminar or a Meetup group with like-minded individuals, sign up for a class. Or ask around until you find a role model who has achieved the same goal.

LESSON 41: MASTERING COMMUNICATION 108
- Action: Make a commitment to improve your command of language, and become a better communicator.

LESSON 42: RECONNECTING WITH YOUR SPIRITUALITY 110
- Action: Remove a distraction or commitment from your life to make time to reconnect with your spirituality.

LESSON 43: ESCAPE THE HERD 113
- Action: Get away from it all, and write down ideas that pop into your head.

LESSON 44: IT'S ABOUT TIME! 116
- Action: Take action by using your personal calendar to schedule meaningful commitments.

LESSON 45: DON'T BE SO PRACTICAL 118
- Action: Do something impractical that gets you closer to your goal.

LESSON 46: VALUING YOUR TIME 121
- Action: Evaluate your time usage.

LESSON 47: KEEP ADDING TO YOUR LIFE LIST 124
- Action: Evaluate your life list and add at least three things to it.

LESSON 48: CHERISH YOUR ACCOMPLISHMENTS 126
- Action: Make a list of the things you've already accomplished.

LESSON 49: INVEST IN YOURSELF 128
- Action: Choose one self-indulgent investment of time.

LESSON 50: AN ATTITUDE OF GRATITUDE 130
- Action: Make a list of the things you've learned and ways you've grown.

CONCLUSION 132
- Recap of Lessons Learned From John Goddard

INTRODUCTION

THE LIFE AND LESSONS OF JOHN GODDARD

No matter how you view it, John Goddard (author of *The Survivor: 24 Spine-Chilling Adventures on the Edge of Death*) lived an extraordinary life. Since his page on Wikipedia categorizes him as an "adventurer, explorer, author, and lecturer," it would have to be remarkable.

Not one of those achievements was an easy task to accomplish. For example, he wouldn't have been able to take one or two trips abroad and call himself an explorer. To the contrary: He had to push himself out of his comfort zone, believe in himself when no others would, and bet on himself, which is exactly what he remarkably – and literally – did at the tender age of 15.

On one eventful rainy afternoon he was in the kitchen and overheard his parents talking to a friend in the next room. "I wish I was John's age again," the friend said, noting how there were many things he would have accomplished if given another chance. "I wish I could start over."

Goddard resolved then and there not to have those kinds of regrets when he was that age. So he took out a yellow legal pad and wrote down 127 specific life goals that included traversing the entire length of the 4,132-mile Nile River, scaling Mount Kilimanjaro in Tanzania, learning to fence, running a five-minute mile, lighting a match with a .22 rifle, visiting the birthplace of his grandfather [Goddard], and playing Debussy's *Claire de Lune* on the piano.

The rest, as they say, is history.

He not only accomplished almost all of those goals, but another 400 he set along the way, including defeating prostate cancer.

I was first introduced to John through the pages of the first edition of *Chicken Soup for the Soul*. The story of his life list that I read there struck me so much that I immediately created my own list of things to do, and one of those things was to meet John Goddard.

It was several years later and I thought I had located him by researching the Internet. I made a note of his phone number and a vow that I would call him on my next trip to Southern California.

That trip was to come in early 2006 when my wife and I made plans to attend the National Championship game that year to watch her beloved Texas Longhorns defeat Southern Cal in one of the most memorable games in college football history.

About a month before the trip I mustered all the courage I had and dialed the number I had found for John. I wasn't surprised that my call went to an answering machine and I left a message that I'd thought about before the call. Included in the message was the mention that I was an acquaintance of Mark Victor Hansen (co-creator of the Chicken Soup series that had featured John's story).

I was surprised by how quickly he returned the call and blown away by how humble and approachable he was during our conversation. I told him that we'd be in Pasadena shortly and that I'd like to buy him lunch. Instead of meeting at a restaurant, he suggested we come by his house – WOW!

What I originally thought would be a half an hour to one-hour visit turned into hours as he showed us some of the thousands of artifacts and mementos he had from his multitude of pursuits. We agreed to talk again soon and over the next few years I would get the opportunity to spend some incredible time with him.

He appeared twice on my television show, Goals 2 Go. He wowed the audience with his stories at a three-day event we sponsored in L.A. He even included Lisa and me in a very intimate group of friends he selected to hike the San Gabriel Mountains one weekend. It's some of the most memorable days I've ever had.

John passed to the next great adventure in 2013, but he didn't leave the Earth without also leaving a tremendous legacy behind. Called by some the "real Indiana Jones," Goddard's enduring message is clear: if you have the guts to make real, definable goals and the fortitude to stick with them, then you can do anything—and become anyone—that you want.

What's remarkable about his story is that he didn't complete his *entire* list. Some of his goals—like exploring the moon—remained elusive to Goddard. Yet if you were to review his Life List today, you would find it a catalogue of realized dreams, daring achievements, and ultimately, a life well lived.

That's the message of John Goddard: to live your life as *you* see fit, not to listen to what the naysayers and even your own fears would have you believe is possible. Throughout this book we'll explore 50 lessons I learned that helped Goddard achieve his goals—and can help you live a life of similar richness, wonder, and achievement.

(Note: Each lesson is followed by an action step or steps to take to help you develop and achieve your life list. It is the intention of this book that by the end of Lesson 50 you will have not only learned more about John Goddard, but how you too can live a life of great adventure, whatever that will mean for you.)

(**Attention All Eagle Eyes**: We've had a number of people proof this book before we released it to you, but there is a chance you might spot something that was missed. If you find a typo or other obvious error, please send it to us. And if you're the first one to report it we'll send you a free gift! Send to: corrections@laurenzanapress.com)

Lesson 1

DEFINING BLISS

If life was easy to figure out, the formula would be simple: Just copy John Goddard's life list and get to work. But we all know life is complicated and things can sometimes get in the way of our accomplishments. Goals that meant something to him (like visiting a movie studio, circumnavigating the globe, piloting the world's fastest airplane, exploring the Great Barrier Reef, etc.) might not mean the same to you.

Even if you were to have his list and achieve those goals, you most likely wouldn't receive the same satisfaction and fulfillment he received from his achievements. Which is why it's critically important to be clear that *your* life list should be about what makes *you* happy. Otherwise, what's the point?

When John's parents' friend said he wished he could be John's age again, there was unhappiness and discontent in his voice. It wasn't that he hadn't explored the Congo or that he hadn't made it to the moon; it was that he hadn't pursued his dreams to the fullest and felt it was too late to try.

It doesn't matter whether you want to become a bestselling author or an internationally recognized pianist; they both boil down to the same result: A way for you to live a life rich with bliss, excitement, happiness and fulfillment.

But you need to define what "bliss" means to you. *Your* bliss doesn't belong to your parents ... your siblings ... your friends or acquaintances ... or even your enemies. It belongs *to you and only you*. Fully comprehending this concept will help you personalize your life list according to what you want to accomplish.

Every time you mention a goal you may encounter opposition from people who don't share or understand your aspirations. They'll wonder why you're putting in so much effort to do things that to them seem pointless, irrelevant, and idiotic. What they don't realize is that bliss alone is a worthy goal to achieve.

Of course it's tough to experience bliss on a consistent basis! If it wasn't, everyone would be in a constant state of ecstasy. The truth is, although a perpetual state of happiness is difficult to achieve, once it's reached it has the same sense of achievement and fulfillment as reaching any goal.

So before you move on to the next section, please remember that your personalized journey is about what makes you happy. Don't walk in someone else's shoes (you need to walk in your own that fit comfortably), and don't walk the path your fears would have you take. If you follow your own compass you'll discover that bliss was there all along.

Action: **Answer six important questions, and then create a life list that excites you.**

You may have already written a bucket list (the movie "The Bucket List" with Morgan Freeman and Jack Nicholson really brought it into the fore). But the list you're going to develop from the upcoming exercises is going to be highly personalized and tightly tailored to enhance your enjoyment and sense of fulfillment.

Instead of regurgitating old goals, you need to wipe the slate clean. Put even the wildest or most ridiculous answers in a bullet point list to keep them organized.

Don't worry about how simple or complex they are, and don't worry if you'll actually accomplish them. Answering these questions will help you craft your list of things you want to achieve during your lifetime.

Ready? Set? Go!

Question 1:

- What were your dreams and aspirations when you were a child?
- What ideas and adventures excited you?
- As you list them watch for "grown-up" versions of these seeds of enthusiasm.

Question 2:

- What are the goals and experiences you should have on your bucket list? (Don't include things that don't excite you or that feel obligatory. For example, you may think of including running a marathon or participating in a triathlon just because you think it's a typical goal to have. But if you hate physical exertion like running you should cross it off your list. Who cares if other people get great satisfaction from accomplishing that particular goal? Remember, your list needs to be filled with things that make you happy.)

Question 3:

- What are your wildest dreams at this point in time? Include ideal living spaces (a loft in Paris, a cabana on the beach, a bungalow in Monterey); job positions (a programmer for Google, starting your own business, personal assistant to a famous life coach); travel (a cruise to Antarctica, spending a month in Italy in a villa, walking the entire length of the Great Wall of China); and relationships (finding your perfect mate, raising children, having loving friends and family).

Question 4:

- What are simple acts that bring you the greatest pleasure? Include things like food, sex, watching reruns, eating ice cream in the park – anything you can incorporate into a larger goal.

Question 5:

- If you could do anything you desired (and there were no limitations), what would it be this year? In five years? In ten years? And if you want to be ambitious, in 20 years or more?

Question 6:

- If you found out you only had a year to live, what things would you be sure to do in the next 365 days?

Now, with ruthless abandon, go through everything you've written down from all six questions. As you carefully think about each answer, ask yourself : Will pursuing and ultimately accomplishing this truly make me happy? If the answer is no, strike it off the list.

You'll be finished with this exercise when every single goal that remains makes you tingle with anticipation.

Lesson 2

THINK OUTSIDE THE BOX

What Would John Goddard Do?

Thinking "inside" the box is one of the most dangerous things you can do to prevent achieving goals. Okay, that's a total exaggeration since it's obviously more dangerous to go skiing in the middle of a Rocky Mountain avalanche or BASE (Building-Antenna-Span-Earth) jump from the top of the Empire State Building.

But if you don't want to end up regretting your life, then thinking "inside" the box is one of the most important mindsets to avoid.

It's hard to define exactly what "the box" is, but it will resonate when you realize what that means for you. When people try to put you in a box, it's usually based on what they're comfortable with in their own lives: a steady job, a white picket fence, a two-car garage, kids and dogs – everything the American Dream says they're supposed to pursue and win.

If you completed Lesson 1 and have started thinking about what gives you the greatest sense of bliss, you might have stumbled onto something very profound: That the road you're on to fulfillment won't always be smooth.

Blazing a new path means thinking outside conventional wisdom (the box). Goddard knew he wanted to be an adventurer and to share his knowledge with people. At first, he was thinking within the box by assuming he could land a lecturing job at a university and still have the time to explore the world. But he quickly found the world doesn't work that way. So in order to accomplish both lofty goals, he had to carve his own path by thinking outside the box.

What did Goddard end up doing? He created his own job and went on the lecture circuit. Rather than speaking in a crowded university hall, he booked his own speeches and found an audience for his material, which is a classic example of thinking outside the box.

So when confronted with an obstacle, ask yourself **what would John Goddard do**? He learned at a very young age to switch his mindset from "I can't achieve my goal" to "I may not be able to achieve my goal along this particular path, but there may be another path more suitable for me." Therefore, the difference between a negative thinker and a positive realist is the realist knows there are options available to achieve their goals.

If you think outside the "box" of your life, you're bound to find conventional or unconventional ways to achieve your goals. If you give up and give in, you'll find yourself walking the well-beaten path to regret.

Action: **Identify your goal, and take a radical step to achieve it.**

If you've been studying your life list, you might be thinking it's not long enough. If to this point you haven't achieved many or any of your goals, you've probably been routinely living your life and may have given up on your dreams.

So the lesson in this chapter is to choose one goal and take steps you've never taken before to achieve it. The catch is it needs to be something you wouldn't have tried in the past as it felt out of reach or too daunting.

First, you need to review your life list to find goals that would mesh well together, or if there are any you can pursue at the same time. Will any of the goals build upon one another or feed into your overall success?

Now ask yourself how a traditional (in-the-box) and a radical (outside-the-box) thinker would achieve these goals. The following is an example of thinking outside of the box:

John and Kate are married with two elementary school children. Although they both work full-time, they've been dreaming of traveling the world. Instead of waiting until the kids are grown, they decided not to wait and approached their employers about working remotely for a year.

They withdrew their kids from public school, registered as a homeschooled family, subleased their house, and chose six different locations around the world they wanted to travel to.

They rented inexpensive apartments and spent two months in each locale working their jobs and exposing their children to new cultures while home schooling them in what they needed to pass their tests.

The end result? Everyone in the family learned new ways of life, grew from their experiences, and made memories that can never be replaced.

Your goal choice doesn't need to be as radical as John and Kate's. But if traveling around the world is one of your life list goals you could take one or more of the following outside-the-box steps:

- Make an appointment with your boss to discuss traveling for work or working in another part of the world.

- Discuss this wild idea with your partner, which will set the wheel of change in motion.

- Research places you'd like to visit, and include important details like costs of housing, language you need to learn, visa or passport requirements.

- Then renew your passport or get a new one, or apply for a foreign work visa.

Whatever your goal is, taking steps completely out of your comfort zone will pull you out of your rut and open your mind to new possibilities.

Lesson

DON'T JUST DREAM IT — BE IT!

"Excellence is an art won by training and habituation; we do not act rightly because we have virtue or excellence, but rather we have these because we have acted rightly..." ~ Aristotle

In other words, dreaming you're there will not get you there.

It's common for people to fantasize about their own specialness, and to believe their dreams can become realities simply because they want them to. But the truth is, dreaming about a goal is only the first step to achieving it. You must also acquire the characteristics, knowledge, and skills of someone who has already achieved that goal.

Consider a young author who has never been published. They may be very talented, and dream of being the next Ernest Hemingway or Martha Gellhorn. But if all they did was dream about finishing a novel or to hope someone discovers their work, then they probably will be waiting a very long time to see their dream come to fruition (or maybe not ever, and that should scare the heck out of you!)

But if that young person believed they were already an author rather than dreaming about becoming one, they would write every day and start submitting their stories to publishers, newspapers, or have an online blog.

If they behave like the writer they wanted to be, rather than just fantasizing about being one, their dream would begin to manifest into a reality. People would begin to read their work and respond to it. Even a rejection letter would serve a purpose by letting them know something needs to change if they are to be published.

The moral of this example is you need to acquire the characteristics of a goal achiever rather than a goal dreamer.

Many of John Goddard's goals on his life list required a good deal of action. Could he have dreamt his way into riding an elephant? Of course not! An elephant didn't just walk up to his front door and ask if he needed a ride.

Goddard actively sought out an elephant (and a camel, an ostrich, and a bronco) to achieve his goals. He couldn't "dream" them into existence without giving reality a little nudge in the right direction.

This isn't to say you should never dream, because dreaming is a form of bliss. But if they only remain dreams and no action is taken to make them a reality, then you can become that person saying at the end of their life, "I wish I could be young again to do the things on my list." So fill in the missing pieces of the puzzle, and become a goal achiever like John Goddard who lived a very big, very fulfilling life.

Action: **Make an identity dream board or mind map. Then adapt to your new persona.**

You've written a life list, identified a goal you wish to achieve, and taken a radical first step. Now you need to take on the identity of a person who has achieved the same kind of goal.

For example: a runner is disciplined, exercises often, knows about running gear, techniques, how their body functions and its limitations. And above all, they run.

For this exercise you'll need to assume an identity necessary to become the person who achieves their life goals. You'll do this by creating a dream board upon which you will place pictures, words, and images that symbolize your new identity.

Place the name (i.e., sculptor, Internet marketing guru, minister, marathon runner, champion boxer, international traveler, etc.) of your new persona in the center of the board. Now place words and images from magazines, the Internet, or ones you've drawn around your new identity.

If this feels awkward, you can use an online mind mapping tool and place your new identity title in the center bubble, and then use the surrounding bubbles to describe your new persona.

Then study the dream board or mind map, and visualize yourself after adopting this new persona.

The person you've been, up to this point, may not have achieved many adventures (otherwise, you probably wouldn't be reading this book). So taking on a new persona is like trying on a costume to portray a character in a play. Life is your stage, and you'll be performing on it from here on out.

Lesson 4

MAKE FRIENDS WHEREVER YOU GO

If you achieved your goals, but there was no one around to share in your joy, how much would those goals be worth? You know the answer: They wouldn't be worth as much as you had hoped.

Not only is it important for you to have family and friends to share your dreams with, you need to make new relationships during the journey to achieve your goals.

Part of what made John Goddard's life so rich is that he came up with goals that couldn't be achieved alone. Because he needed assistance from others to achieve those things on his life list, he was frequently in a position to make new friends and acquaintances. After a new goal was achieved, his life was richer vis-à-vis those experiences and for the new friends he made along the way.

Those words "along the way" are very powerful. Most of your time achieving goals is going to be spent somewhere "along the way." So if you can't find a way to make the journey fun, exciting, worthwhile, and valuable, you're going to be spending a considerable portion of your life being miserable.

However, if you're able to make those "along the way" portions more meaningful, your life as a whole will be richer and this includes making friends along the way. (In subsequent sections, I'll address how your friends and family can be a hindrance while tackling new goals.)

Getting rid of negative influences won't be easy unless you have a positive support system that is created from meeting like-minded people.

What kinds of friends do you think John Goddard made when he was scaling the Matterhorn or exploring the Congo? He made friends who shared a similar excitement for adventure and wonder with the world. It was those people who not only made his life richer, but afforded him the opportunity to repay their kindnesses in turn.

After all, the influence we have on others and the experiences we can share with them – and vice versa – is what life is all about. As you get older and find yourself reflecting on your past, you'll ruminate not only on experiences and events but the people you shared them with, which is why it's so critical to make the right friends along the way.

Action: **Initiate with one positive, inspiring person; and pull away from one negative, sabotaging person.**

Nothing kills the spirit more than a naysayer. If you've been sharing your goals with others, you'll probably be faced with people who fall into three categories:

1. Those who actively support your ideas.

2. Those who become barriers to your ideas and sabotage them (the naysayers).

3. Those who are neutral.

During this lesson you'll disconnect from the most negative person in your social circle, and proactively initiate a new relationship with the most positive or inspiring person in or outside your circle.

Your action may look like any or all of the following:

- Ask a person who inspires you to correspond via email, texting, Skype or in person.

- Join a local group and/or online forum of like-minded people who want to achieve the same goal(s) you're pursuing.

- Tell one friend that you are wholeheartedly pursuing your new goal, and won't be able to do things you usually do together (or the very least as often).

- Ask someone to be an accountability/inspiration partner so you have someone to discuss goals with each day.

Therefore, this exercise is to decrease the number of naysayers, and increase the number of positive inspirational people who will support you as a goal achiever.

Lesson 5

MAKE A DIFFERENCE

No human being wants to feel irrelevant. No matter how small their dreams are, they want to feel they've affected the world in some positive way. Not everyone wants to be the president of the United States, but they do want to impact others in some profound way.

Making a difference requires venturing off the beaten path (going back to stepping out of the box), or attempting something no one has tried before. Making a difference means putting ego on the line, risking a reputation, and taking chances.

Consider Jackie Robinson, the first African-American player in Major League Baseball (MLB). Robinson's life was filled with hatred, bigotry, and resistance at every turn in the road. But without his substantial sacrifices, the game of baseball wouldn't be where it is today.

Making a difference doesn't mean it has to be earth-shaking. It can be something small like taking an hour to coach children or to work in a soup kitchen. The point of making a difference is to create a positive change in someone's life.

John Goddard made a difference in people's lives because they were inspired to use the same strategies to turn their lives around, which is why making a difference boils down to the act of giving.

Actions don't exist in a vacuum. It's hard to make much of a difference to people's lives if you're focused solely on yourself. In order to become relevant, you need to find ways to make the world a better place and enhance the lives of others.

Action: **Give generously of your time or resources to someone who has the same goals.**

As you pursue your goal, you'll often find like-minded individuals who want to achieve something similar, but are further behind or less capable. Perhaps you want to become a painter, so you enroll in classes to help you perfect your technique.

Then you find out your niece also longs to paint. Not only will you improve your skills, you'll gain great personal satisfaction by inviting her to paint with you (or teach her) on a regular basis.

Your exercise is to give inspiration, partnership and/or resources to someone interested in the same area of interest you're pursuing. Your generosity will reinforce your new role while moving you closer to your goal.

Lesson

IMAGINE IT'S ALREADY DONE

You're probably wondering what kind of help imagining it is already done can be to you. After all, if you imagined something was already done, wouldn't you lose your motivation for doing it?

The truth is, your imagination is a powerful tool for helping you achieve your goals. John Goddard said he visualized "everything panning out" to cultivate a positive attitude and anticipation that might not have occurred but for his intense mental preparation. When you're exploring raw and dangerous territories like the Congo or the Amazon (or even driving in traffic), it helps to have confidence that everything is indeed going to "pan out."

Of course it can be difficult to stay inspired all of the time. But simply imagining that a goal is already accomplished can invigorate you with the same drive you had at the beginning of your journey. Which in turn will help you commit to your goals with a renewed sense of passion.

Imagining that something is already done can also alert you to blind spots within your own strategies. For example, if you had a goal of playing a piano piece and imagined you already knew how to play it you might think, *Wait a minute. I haven't bought the sheet music to learn it. Guess I'd better do that first.*

Imagining something is already done can prime your mind for success the same way you prime an engine before starting it. It's important not to think of yourself as someone who's destined to fail. If that's the way you truly view yourself, you're bound to find some way to make it happen. Isn't that what they call a self-fulfilling prophecy?

You've probably met someone who was determined to come up with reasons for why their dreams **weren't** panning out, no matter how supportive you were. But you want to be the person who keeps finding reasons why your goals **will** pan out.

The key to this is no matter what your expectations, you'll usually find some way to make reality match them. If you have negative expectations, you'll generally find the negative in each situation. So you want this human instinct to work for you, not against you.

Action: **Spend time fantasizing about your success.**

This exercise is about fantasizing about success while actively taking action towards achieving your goal. Visualization is what helps Russian Olympic athletes stay focused on their training, so you'll want to visualize your success down to minute details.

Daydream about it. Practice your acceptance speech. Imagine telling your kids about your adventures. Envision being interviewed by a news reporter or cashing that first big check.

Lesson

MAKE EVERY MINUTE COUNT

John Goddard had a very ambitious life list that included exploring many of the world's biggest rivers, studying the natives of countries all over the globe, climbing mountains like Mount Kilimanjaro and Mt. Rainier, and composing music. Looking at just how vast his list was, your question might not be how he achieved those goals, but how he ever found the time with his busy schedule and personal responsibilities.

Goddard was able to accomplish a great deal by incorporating an important premise into his desires: Everyone has the same amount of seconds in their minutes, minutes in their hours, and hours in their days. It's what they do with their time that makes the difference. The key then to proper time management is to cram as much as you possibly can into the minutes you're allotted every day.

Goddard was amazed at how many hours people waste on inconsequential things when there were so many other things they could be doing. So he avoided time wasters in order to fit more meaningful accomplishments into his life.

Stay Focused on Your Goal

You're likely not going to look back at your life on your deathbed and say, "I wish I had watched more television," or "I should have spent my time aimlessly surfing the Internet."

Most likely you're going to wish you had fit more meaningful minutes into your days to make your life more substantive.

In order to make every minute count, you need to shift your intention like John Goddard did. Whether you're focusing on one goal at the moment, or assessing your entire life list, you need to determine what you want to accomplish and start devising a strategy to achieve your goals.

Because time is finite, spending more time on your goals means you'll have to spend less time somewhere else. Nothing well-earned is without some sort of sacrifice. Carefully watch the amount of time you spend at the computer, in front of the television, texting friends, or reading books that serve no purpose.

This doesn't mean you have to give up everything you like to do, but you do need to keep focused and on-target. Ultimately, you'll thank yourself for your efforts. Because no matter what you do, or how much you wish it were otherwise, time is going to pass. So you need to focus on making an impact now in order to prevent regrets down the road.

Action: **Identify and eliminate two hours of wasted time.**

This exercise is to first figure out what you've been doing with your time in order to see where it's being wasted.

Keep a daily log of what you do every single waking hour for two full work days and one weekend. Don't skip any hours or things you think are inconsequential, because you want to be able to recognize where you're wasting time.

Then go back through the log and highlight at least two hours of repetitive non-essential things that are obviously eating your time. You may realize that you're actually spending four hours in front of the television instead of one; or two hours playing Scrabble on your iPad; or way too much time on Facebook.

You might find you're a putterer or an over-achiever (believe it or not, over-achievers can waste a lot of time by over-organizing lists or doing too many inconsequential tasks during a day just to fulfill the need of feeling productive).

Rid your life of time wasters by announcing your commitment to do so to a partner, friend, or an online forum.

Lesson

LEARN FROM YOUR DISASTERS

It's a fact of life that disasters happen. And no matter how prepared you are for them, they'll almost always catch you off guard. But successful people know how to use disasters as learning opportunities and to their advantage.

People are often more prepared after hurricanes, tornados, floods, forest fires, and stock market crashes because they've learned what they lacked, and find ways to have those things in place in the event of future disasters.

You should expect no less from yourself.

Having an attitude of preparedness is helpful because it can build your confidence. If you learn from your mistakes and disastrous moments you can confidently handle things that go wrong.

John Goddard confidently rode an Ostrich because he knew that if something bad had happened he'd use it as a learning opportunity instead of feeling like a failure.

It was also risky to explore the Great Barrier Reef in turbulent waters. But if he hadn't found the courage or hadn't had the tools to be prepared in the event of a disaster, he never would have been able to photograph a 300-pound clam at the bottom of the Pacific Ocean. Through his training and mistakes, he learned what he needed to have in place to keep himself safe and alive and have an adventure at the same time!

Concerning disaster Goddard said, "I've always learned from it. It's always been exciting, and in some instances enjoyable because I'm using my God-given capacities – that we all have – and potential, and I was winning. I wasn't set back by discouragement."

Have Realistic Perspectives

It's important to keep the term "disaster" in proper perspective. Is it a disaster if you get a rejection letter from a publisher? Absolutely not! One rejection letter doesn't make you a failure. It just gives you more opportunities to hone your skills at writing perfect query letters. Every rejection is an opportunity to excel.

Is it a disaster if you don't win that cartoon caption contest you keep entering? No, it isn't. There's always next week, and the week after that. You keep submitting until you do win.

Is it a disaster if you didn't get accepted to the school you want? Emphatically no! There are plenty of schools that can help you on your path to achieving your dreams, and you just need to find the right fit. It may be a blessing that Stanford turned you down when you really wanted to go to a design school in New York. As they say, when one door closes another one opens.

Surviving a disaster fosters confidence. Once you've made it through a disaster, and learned what to do the next time, you can handle anything.

So how will you handle your next disaster?

Action: **Make a list of possible disasters that could stop you from meeting your goals.**

You've probably heard of preppers and survivors – people who stock up on food, water and survival supplies in preparation of a natural disaster or economic collapse.

This exercise is to help you survive setbacks by identifying and being prepared for disasters that have stopped you or brought you to your knees in the past. Knowing what to expect, and having tools in your arsenal to overcome adversities, can help you reach your goals faster and with less obstacles.

Therefore, you're to create a disaster avoidance and recovery plan, and share it with an accountability partner, online forum, or friend who will help you when you hit roadblocks.

Lesson

DISASTERS CAN BE BLESSINGS

In the previous lesson you saw that John Goddard used disasters as learning experiences. And yes, a disaster *can* be a blessing.

At first glance, the word *blessing* seems like wishful thinking in this context. After all, they wouldn't call it a disaster if it wasn't something calamitous. So how on earth could a disaster be a blessing when the very word seems to suggest it's just the opposite?

As John Goddard would say, it's a question of confidence. He faced tremendous obstacles while exploring the world, including suffering from an appendicitis attack when he was far away from proper medical care. So he came up with a plan to operate on himself, and instructed his friend on what to do in case he passed out. Fortunately, he never had to go to such lengths, but it was in the planning to do something where Goddard found his confidence.

You too can find confidence and self-belief from a disaster, and all it takes is one or two split-second decisions to realize your true potential in these situations. To Goddard, doing well during a disaster was a matter of "not feeling sorry for myself, and not having excuses."

Even if you don't have an immediate answer to solving the problem, you can still find the best of yourself when faced with adversity. You can avoid self-pity and excuses and take action, even if the action seems like it won't have any effect on the outcome. What matters is that you do the best you can, even in the direst of circumstances.

Goddard ended up with a very bad tapeworm after one of his excursions, and rather than feel sorry for himself he named it Rodney. It was his positive attitude (and a good sense of humor) that defined Goddard's courage and ability to deal with the circumstances.

So how do you fare in times of difficulty? Are you quick to give in to self-pity? Or do you look for the blessing of self-confidence that comes out of handling disasters the right way? First, you find courage, then you take action, and soon after you'll realize the blessing.

Action: **Every night write down two blessings that happen each day, and focus on how the good of those blessings will carry you toward your goals.**

You've been writing down one thing you did right each day. So this exercise is about also writing down two blessings that occur during the day.

By counting your blessings and affirming your ability to handle pressure, you'll build positivity toward achieving your goals.

Lesson 10

FOCUS ON THE GOOD

Focus is like having a super power. Not only does a magnifying glass make small objects larger, but it can focus light into a raging fire! It's just the matter of the intention of its purpose. Every human being possesses the ability to focus, and if they don't use their ability properly or with proper intention, it can prevent them from attaining their goals.

John Goddard liked to focus on the good of the goals he wanted to accomplish instead of things to fear or to avoid. By focusing on where he wanted to go, and the positive results, he used his "super power" to his benefit.

You too can utilize your "super power" by asking questions prior to your journey. Instead of asking "What can I do to avoid being unhappy?" you should ask, "What goal can I achieve that will make me happy?" See how that switched it from sabotaging your life list to making it a possibility?

You might think those questions sound the same, and to a mathematician two negatives can make a positive. But in the world of mental focus they're polar opposites. Look at them again and you'll see "avoid" versus "achieve." Now do you get it?

Let's say you're setting a travel goal and trying to figure out what country to visit that will make you the happiest. Saying "I don't want to travel to Canada" might mean you've eliminated one country from the list. But about 99% of the other countries remain, so you haven't accomplished anything other than eliminating one tiny dot from the map.

However, if you say, "Traveling to France would make me happy," you're eliminating 99% of the other countries which is far more positive, and has helped you make a definitive decision about where to start organizing travel plans.

Applying this approach to life in general, you'll have better results if you focus on what's good rather than avoid what's bad, which will require you to become more specific about your goals. John Goddard's life list was packed with realistically achievable and very specific actionable goals he could cross off as he attained them. The Congo – check! The Amazon – check! The Great Wall of China – check! Check! Check!

It's known that he had around 111 checkmarks on his bucket list by the time he died (out of 127 on his original list to which he added about 400 more, which is pretty astounding!). Therefore, his goal of exploring the Amazon River was far more positive and specific than a goal of "avoid becoming stagnant." Do you see the difference?

When you focus on what's good you can make it specific, intensify it, and turn it into a real-world goal. But when you focus on avoiding the bad, all you end up getting is more, well...bad.

Action: **Post sticky notes where you can frequently see them documenting good experiences you've had.**

You're bound to have encountered the good and bad about things as you've begun actualizing your goals. So you need to stay hyper-focused solely on the good if you want to be able to check them off your list.

This exercise is to go through your efforts to-date, and record everything positive that has happened thus far. Write them as bullet points on the sticky notes, and place them everywhere as constant reminders of your achievements.

Add more notes as you think of more accomplishments, study them as you pass by, and you'll come to see a pattern of positive results you can carry forth while pursuing your list.

Lesson 11

CREATE VISUALIZATION TOOLS

You may have heard of using visualization as a tool for getting what you want out of life, and thought it was some nonsense passed down by shamans and seers throughout the ages. However, it is a practice that's been around since the beginning of time, and has been used by millions of people to create reality from a very abstract concept such as literally think and ye shall receive.

In the case of John Goddard the power of visualization was very real. He said that when writing his life list he imagined himself accomplishing every single one of his goals from inception to completion. For example, he imagined visiting the source of the Nile and all the excitement and revelations that would entail, and ultimately he was able to do just that.

To Goddard, visualization was the process of taking a goal from a dream to reality. Instead of simply daydreaming, he used visualization to imagine how the trip would go, which was the first step in his planning process. Eventually, he made real plans to accomplish every goal on his list because he thought them into being a reality.

Visualization can work equally as well for you, but it's important to draw a very clear distinction between visualization and mere daydreaming.

Daydreaming is often used as a tool to escape, a way to fantasize about something without putting in the effort toward its completion. Of course, it's great fun to think about faraway places and exotic adventures. But daydreaming won't make something happen as it's based strictly on a wish and not the possibility of reality. After you're done daydreaming, you can feel despondent and isolated because you've returned to reality and the dream is still a dream.

On the other hand, visualization is an active sort of daydreaming in which you grab the reins and tell your imagination where you want to go. Then after you're done visualizing, you feel energized and happier because you've made a constructive step towards accomplishing your goal. You've seen it happen, you know what it feels like to be there, you've seen sights and heard sounds. You've thought it; ergo, it can become reality.

Goddard said that when you take control of your daydream you essentially lose the ability to be bored. Suddenly your life becomes interactive (a form of virtual reality) where you can pretty much do anything your mind can create. All that remains to be done is to carry out the plans you've visualized into reality.

Isn't that an exciting way to look at the world around you? Instead of feeling you have a boring existence and there's no way out, you can begin to look at your dreams as Tinker Toys and Play-Doh to create all sorts of realities. This is a far more powerful way of looking at the reality around you, and will end up giving you a lot more power over the direction of your life.

Action: **Create an inspirational image, and put it where you can see it often.**

Visualization isn't daydreaming as it requires focus (sort of like meditation), and total faith or belief that something can happen. Start visualizing with intention and you'll feel enthused, prepared, and confident in your ability to achieve your dreams.

This exercise is to choose something that symbolizes the achievement of your goal (or more than one if a combination of visualizations helps you to better see your goal), and place it where you can see it on a regular basis.

For example, you might choose:

- A check written out to you for one million dollars (you can print out one on your computer, or hand-write one).
- A publishing contract for your novel with your name on it.
- A picture of the top of Mount Everest (you could even Photoshop a photo of you standing there).
- Running in the Boston Marathon.
- Winning a local quilt-making contest.
- Teaching the deaf at an orphanage.
- Even something as simple as a victory garden in your back yard.

Then visualize the actions:

- Someone writing your name on the check and handing it to you.
- An agent signing the publishing contract and handing it to you.
- The photographer shooting the photo of you standing on the top of Mount Everest.
- Breaking through the finish line tape at the Boston Marathon.
- Receiving the blue ribbon for the best quilt in the show while shaking hands with the mayor.
- Standing next to a blackboard at an orphanage to witness the first time a deaf child wrote their name.
- Clipping and gathering fresh flowers from your victory garden for your dinner party.

Visualize it ... believe it ... put it into action ... make it a reality.

Lesson 12

FALL IN LOVE WITH YOUR DREAMS

Defining Your Passion

Even though the question "do you have passion?" should be easy to respond with a yes or a no, many people vacillate about their answer because passion means different things to different people. And they really may not know if they have passion because they've yet to understand what that means to them. They want to believe they have passion for their dreams, and they may be taking concrete steps toward achieving them without fully understanding what they're passionate about.

If you find yourself hesitating to answer that question, it may be time to reassess your goals (which you can do by falling in love with your dreams).

Why is passion so critical to achieving goals? Because it inspires you to keep going no matter the obstacles and setbacks. Passion is the fire that fuels purpose. And like with focus it can ignite your desires and dreams, and keep them burning for a very long time.

John Goddard said, "If you fail at something, it's still gratifying that you at least attempted it when most people won't even make that first stab at something they want to do."

If you fall in love with your dreams, then even the act of attempting to do them can be extremely gratifying. It won't even matter if you succeed or fail (although if you fail, you'll be motivated to continue until you succeed).

For example, let's say you want to be a Hollywood actor. Did you know that many people celebrate when they get an audition? They're in love with their dream and have worked hard to jump through difficult hoops just to get to that stage. And with visualization (and of course a little luck and being in the right place), they can send up balloons and clink champagne glasses when they finally get the part (from visualization to making the dream a reality).

Get On the Right Path

You need to feel positive about your action steps, which is when you'll know you've fallen in love with your dream and that you're on the right path.

In many ways passion is the opposite of apathy. Even though apathy doesn't feel good or bad, the actual void caused by the lack of caring or passion is what defines it. Apathy is the first stop on the road to depression, and it's at that point when you have an opportunity to care about something enough to make it happen and go right to happiness or turn left to years of regret.

Falling in love with your dreams will inspire you to action, and to overcoming your fear of failure. Passion makes you feel gratified. And like when you were a kid, passion makes you feel bad that you have to go to sleep at night and have to wait until morning comes.

Action: **Surround yourself with visual aids that inspire you to pursue your goal.**

Passion involves emotions that are often forgotten or set aside as we tenaciously pour ourselves into the pursuit of our goals. When the mind takes over and tucks passion into a corner, hard work seems to be the thing that matters.

This exercise is to find ways to stir your heart and create more passion for your life list. People are visual and auditory creatures. Therefore, you need to devote time every day searching for music, movies, literature or art that inspires you to pursue your goals.

For example:

- If you want to be a dancer, collect photos of ballet dancers from the New York or Russian dance companies, and famous ballerinas or danseurs (male).

- If you want to be an explorer, find photographs by explorers of lands you want to visit.

- If you want to learn to fly an airplane, buy a subscription to a magazine for pilots.

- If you love restoring antique cars, buy posters or books of vintage vehicles.

- If you want to complete an ironman triathlon, find photos of winners crossing the finish line, and/or music that encourages you to push your body to extremes during exercise.

- If you want to start your own business, watch a movie about a famous entrepreneur like Mark Zuckerberg (Facebook), Steve Jobs (Apple), or Donald Trump (Trump Towers).

- If you want to travel internationally, read books, watch videos, or browse websites that vividly describe the places you'd like to visit.

Can't find anything you feel passionate about at the moment? Dig up oldies but goodies from your past, and absorb how they made you feel then and now. Passion doesn't have to be new. Remember, focus is the match that lights the flame, so you need to take the time to appreciate art forms that stir your passion.

Lesson 13

NEVER FEAR FAILURE

Failure is a mindset. In a success-oriented society failure can mean lack of self-worth, so people's failure are often inflicted upon others and become embedded in the psyche.

A parent's failure can prevent a child from becoming famous; an author's failure means they'll discourage others from wanting to write; someone who tried to get into the Olympics and failed may instill such fear in young athletes that they give up.

Again, failure is a mindset, so altering the meaning of failure can mean the difference between achieving/not achieving the life list. Failure needs to be changed from a negative to a positive, and it's all about re-conditioning the mind to think differently.

There are many definitions of failure:

- Not achieving the desired end

- The condition of being insufficient or falling short

- A cessation of proper functioning or performance

- Non-performance of what is requested or expected

- A decline in strength or effectiveness

If you're like everyone else, you've probably failed many times during your life. Maybe you failed on a school or driver's license test. Maybe you asked someone out on a date, and they said they only see you as a friend. Maybe you tried to launch a bottle rocket into the air, but the bottle tipped over and just laid there and sputtered. Maybe you've started more than one business, but for whatever reason they didn't succeed.

Failing feels awful, so you develop a fear of trying again (in essence, you become fearful of fear). If you have a life list but don't have anything checked off, it could be that it's the FEELING you're avoiding and not failing itself.

The fear of failure can block talented and skilled people from pursuing their dreams. Think about how many novels haven't been written because writers feared rejection from publishers (if J. K. Rowling had allowed her fear of rejection to decide her fate, the *Harry Potter* series would never have been written; or the "Rocky" series might not have been filmed because Stallone didn't submit his script). Think about how many people end up alone because they fear rejection from someone who might have otherwise accepted their offer for a date.

Think of how John Goddard might have ended up living a very mundane life if he had allowed fear to prevent him from attempting any of those 127 feats on his life list.

If you fear failure, you'll never take the necessary risks to achieve success. So it's important to develop a healthy relationship with failure, and change your mindset about what failure truly is. When you embrace failure as a "feedback mechanism" rather than as judgment on your self-worth, you'll develop a healthy relationship with failure.

All You Need is One...

When people ridiculed Thomas Edison about all the failure he had while inventing the light bulb, he said, "I have not failed. I've just found 10,000 ways that won't work."

John Goddard said failure means there's always something to be learned by having made the effort. If one thing fails you've learned it can't work that way, so you change your strategy and keep persisting.

Let's say you have a goal of being a cartoonist, so you create a portfolio of cartoons and send it out to syndicates. You get a pile of rejections, and wonder if cartooning was ever what you were meant to do. Your self-worth takes a hit, and you stuff the portfolio into a closet because it reminds you of how painful failure is.

But guess what? **All you need is one** syndicate to buy your cartoons in order to become a cartoonist. **All you need is one** editor to validate your work to feel like you have a chance as a writer. **All you need is one** callback after an audition to get you a lead role in a movie.

You could stack up a million failures, but it only takes one success to change your life. So don't ever give up. Keep looking for that one success that will mean everything. Because measured against the weight of that one success a lifetime of failures can't begin to stack up.

Which is why failing isn't such a bad thing.

Action: **Find a failure-proof mentor.**

Remember that disaster recovery plan you developed? This exercise is about finding a disaster recovery *hero*. In other words, someone who has pursued a goal, failed, recovered and has gone on to achieve success.

For example, let's say you want to write a novel or an eBook. You'll want to find an author who had to write several books before they got published. You could find this person online through a writing forum, their own website or blog, or at a writing group or workshop. Befriend them and ask them to mentor you until you succeed.

Just the sheer act of approaching them in itself is overcoming the fear of failure. People talk themselves out of many things they regret later that they could have done if they had just learned how to conquer their fears. It's the journey, exploration, and final outcome that is the success.

Lesson 14

FACE YOUR FEARS

Like failure, fear can equate to pain. No one wants to be in pain, so they'll go to any length to avoid it.

In addition to his adventuring and exploring, John Goddard was a public speaker. Like many people he had anxiety when speaking in front of a crowd, possibly more than the fear he experienced during his adventures.

Goddard said he had been asked to give a speech to a convention in Utah. Expecting to speak to around 500 people, he learned the audience was closer to 8,000! He recalled shaking uncontrollably and nearly having a panic attack when he saw how huge the crowd was going to be.

While thinking about giving into his fears and skipping the event, he had an epiphany: When they could be doing something else, everyone had given up an evening to come listen to him speak.

So he asked himself, was he prepared to give up because he was afraid? When he realized that fear alone wasn't a valid excuse, he went out on stage in spite of it. During the course of his speech he imagined giving it to just a few people in the audience, which eliminated the impact of how many people were staring at him. The event ended up going extremely well, and the audience responded wonderfully.

That night Goddard hit on an important truth: While fear has a purpose, it shouldn't be given power when it's the only reason for not doing something. There's a stark difference between the kind of fear you feel when facing a black mamba snake in South Africa (real danger), and the kind of fear you feel when giving a speech to an audience (perceived danger).

Facing your fears can teach you a multitude of valuable lessons. For starters, it teaches you self-confidence and self-reliance. But it also strips away the illusion of fear.

In many cases fear happens before an event. For example, when was the last time you felt fear at the conclusion of a speech? Chances are you felt the greatest amount of fear right before a speech – those moments when you were ready to go on stage and worried you might forget your speech or make a mistake. You might be worried the audience won't be receptive to what you have to say, and you see them leaving one by one.

The chances are none of that will ever happen, and your mind has created an unfounded fear instead of the reality that your speech will be greatly accepted and appreciated. Your mindset has sabotaged your efforts even before you step in front of the podium.

It's important to distinguish between **the fear** of the action and **the act** of the action. In most cases taking action isn't as scary as you might have thought, especially when it comes to social fears. So you need to dissect your fears to break them into manageable components. Is it really that hard to give a speech? Is it really difficult to introduce yourself to people? If you've done this on a regular basis, do you usually start to feel confident while giving the speech? And do you love the applause at the end?

General George Patton said he didn't take counsel of his fears (meaning he didn't give into them), which is a great way of approaching your fears. It's fine to experience fear, but it's not fine to allow it to govern your decisions (getting on the stage and giving a successful speech). The next time you feel afraid and want to avoid something, ask yourself if the fear itself is really a valid excuse. What are the real emotions behind your fear?

Franklin Delano Roosevelt said in his first inaugural address as president of the United States: "The only thing we have to fear is fear itself."

The movie, "The King's Speech," showed how King George the VI – a terrible stutterer – overcame his fear of public speaking by working with Australian speech therapist, Lionel Logue, to conquer his speech impediment. Logue helped him realize what he was afraid of, broke it into manageable components, and established a completely new mindset that enabled him to give his famous wartime speech that changed England forever.

Action: **Take action to face your fears.**

If you ask a therapist how to best overcome a fear, they may tell you to identify a situation that makes you feel anxious, then place yourself in that situation for a short amount of time (maybe one or two minutes). The fact that you faced your fear will help you overcome that fear.

Then you celebrate those few minutes that you were in charge of your fear, you had a successful outcome, and now you're ready to embrace something for a longer period of time. This classic technique for overcoming anxiety can be applied to any fears holding you back from accomplishing life goals.

Choose one particular fear that's been getting in the way of your accomplishments. Now find a way to place yourself in that situation for a small amount of time. Tell yourself that you **will** get through the experience, even if it feels unbearable.

Here are some practical examples:

- Maybe as a writer you're fearful of getting rejection letters. So to help you overcome that fear, submit a short piece to a limited number of journals or publishers. Decide ahead of time what you'll do with the rejection letters. Burn them? Shred them and line the hamster's cage? Choosing a way to handle the anticipated rejection with humor and confidence will diffuse the rejection (and won't you be surprised when you get a letter saying they've accepted your piece? The act of facing your fear put you in a position of success without even realizing it.)

- If you're a runner you may be afraid you'll come in last in a race. Sign up for a race you know you can handle, and then run it at a comfortable pace. Remind yourself that finishing the race is far more important than where you place.

- Maybe you have a new business and you're terrified of making cold calls to get clients. Force yourself to make one call – just one – even if you think you're not ready to handle a new client. Just get through the call and don't expect to make a sale or have them hire you for your services. Afterwards, congratulate yourself regardless of the outcome (and again, won't it be grand when they do hire you or want to buy your widget?), and celebrate the fact that you got through the moment, regardless of the results of the action you took.

This exercise is to show you that just the act of facing a fear will get you one step closer to accomplishing your goals.

Lesson 15

IGNORE THE NAYSAYERS

When you alter your life's path and start to become successful, you're going to encounter resistance from people. Oftentimes they are friends, family and colleagues who you thought supported you. But surprise! The naysayers can slip in when you're not looking.

John Goddard's life list was full of unusual goals that attracted naysayers like a magnet. He said he never took them seriously, because he believed his efforts highlighted the naysayers' own insecurities about their accomplishments. A "human quality of jealousy," as he put it, means a lot of people become naysayers for many different reasons.

When relatives said, "You don't want to do that, John," in reference to his propensity to climb, dive, and surf, his response was, "Yes. I really do want to do that" and that was that.

He also encountered many people along the way who told him his goals couldn't be achieved. For instance, when he and his team wanted to explore the Nile River in small canvas and rubber kayaks, people expressed their astonishment and suspicions. "No one's ever done that on the Nile. You'll be stoned. You'll be shot at. You'll die."

Even though his group did get attacked by natives throwing stones, the negative opinions of the naysayers didn't bear out because he and his team finished exploring the Nile and lived to tell about it.

True, the naysayers did give some valid reasons why it couldn't be done. But rather than giving into their fears (and yes, it's usually a fear about what they would or wouldn't do), Goddard ignored them and proceeded on his path. The results? He and his team accomplished what the naysayers never could because they weren't willing to risk, and bought into their own notions of failure before even trying to be successful.

If you live the life naysayers would have you live, you'd be doomed to a boring and meaningless existence. Naysayers often want you to be comfortable, secure, and safe. They don't want you to take risks, to focus very hard on goals, or to live out your dreams. Otherwise, what would be their excuse for not living out their own dreams? If you succeed, you're a constant reminder of their failures, and their comments often stem from pure jealousy.

But you're not living your life for them – **you're living it for you!**

Of course, the most powerful naysayer is the person you see in the mirror. While working to overcome your own self-doubts, you need to work on overcoming other people's doubts and insecurities as they're seldom – if ever – about you. Having faith in yourself does not require that you have faith in other people's opinions.

If you give in to the naysayers and the bubble busters, you won't run the Boston Marathon, climb Mt. Everest, see a sunrise in Belize, or write a children's book. Is that a regret you want at the end of your life?

Action: **Ask a friend or accountability partner to be brutally honest about what they see is holding you back.**

You probably are your biggest obstacle standing in the way of success. You may be allowing your doubts to become self-fulfilling prophesies of failure.

So this exercise is to find someone you trust to hold you accountable to your goals. Then ask them to help you figure out how you can overcome any self-sabotaging actions that are preventing you from achieving your goals.

For example, people who are trying to lose weight may self-sabotage through emotional overeating. If that's your case, your accountability partner can help you devise a plan to stop overeating when tired, bored, lonely, or stressed.

Likewise, people who want to compete in races sometimes over-train to the point of injury. They know they need to slowly build strength and distance, but they push themselves so hard to the point of becoming debilitated. And in essence have "sabotaged" themselves so they won't be able to run longer distances.

Salespeople sometimes tell potential customers why they shouldn't buy a product or use their services, which exposes their doubts and fears instead of projecting competence and confidence.

Are you sabotaging your goals? If so, how can you overcome this tendency to place obstacles in front of your goals?

Lesson 16

TUNE OUT OTHER PEOPLE'S FEARS

In the last two lessons you learned from John Goddard that you shouldn't place too much importance on your fears or on the negative vocalization of naysayers. But there's another influence you're going to have to contend with if you want to see success: Other people's fears.

Other people's fears can make the risks of your own aspirations seem more real, and you start to doubt yourself. "Well, if they feel that I should be afraid, maybe I'm crazy not to be afraid!"

Yes, sometimes people make very good points. But there's also a danger in accepting their fears without first carefully analyzing them, as you'll fall under their sphere of influence rather than influencing yourself. You allow their fears – which may or may not be unfounded – to control your life and sabotage your goals.

John Goddard said that while growing up he quickly learned not to heed people's fears. He became skeptical of naysayers, and took on an attitude of "I know you mean well, but thank you and bug off!" In other words, he listened to what people had to say, let it mull around for a while to see if it had any merit, but ultimately rejected their fears and did what he wanted because it was the right thing for him to do.

Tuning out other people's fears leaves you free to look toward your own dreams with less inhibition and fear of rejection.

You also free yourself of people's limiting beliefs. For instance, why would you listen to an uncle who's never been to Egypt about the dangers of the Nile? Or why would you listen to your cousin saying you should be afraid of public speaking when they've never given a speech in their lifetime?

If you want to unburden yourself of fear, it stands to reason you can't burden yourself with other people's fears. Doing so not only lightens your load, but also helps you defeat the self-doubt that creeps into your subconscious and prevents you from moving forward.

The average man acquires enough fear and self-doubting for several lifetimes, so don't take on negative thoughts and add them to your own. In all likelihood, at this point in life you may have enough of your own to contend with, so you need to put your hands over your ears and tune out everyone else's fears.

Action: **Walk away from negative relationships that bring you down.**

You may discover that some of the people you've partnered with (friends, family, colleagues, peers) say they want to achieve goals, but then fill your head with negativity and excuses about why you can't achieve yours. They want you to buy into their fear in hopes you'll give up and make them happier about their life.

For this exercise you need to examine your social circle for anyone who makes you feel like you can't or shouldn't be pursuing your dreams. Then eliminate or reduce your contact with that person. Negativity has no place in your life while trying to achieve positive goals.

This may require a difficult conversation (explaining why you are moving on to a new training partner, mentor or instructor), or maybe avoidance (becoming too busy to make time for a negative person).

But you need to find a way to make sure their fears don't creep through your window and suffocate you while pursuing your dreams. You want to surround yourself with people who will support, nurture and encourage you on your journey to achieving your bucket list.

Lesson 17

PERSISTENCE PAYS OFF

If there's only one lesson you should take away from John Goddard's experiences let it be persistence, which is one of the most powerful concepts to grasp if you want to achieve success.

President Calvin Coolidge said:

"Nothing in the world can take place of persistence. Talent will not; nothing is more common than unsuccessful men with talent. Genius will not; unrewarded genius is almost a proverb. Education will not; the world is full of educated derelicts. Persistence and determination alone are omnipotent. The slogan 'press on' has solved and always will solve the problems of the human race."

Goddard took this lesson to heart, saying he refused to accept failure. He had flown prop planes in the Air Force, but one of his dreams was to fly a jet-class fighter. When he went to the Air Force, they laughed at him and told him that even professional pilots seldom got that privilege.

But Goddard kept trying to find ways around the obstacle. Eventually, he came up with the idea of filming a documentary about training jet fighter pilots, and approached an Air Force colonel with a detailed, flexible plan to make sure he couldn't say no.

The result? Goddard achieved his dream when he flew with the pilots while making his documentary "Blackout in the Blue." He circumvented failure by approaching the problem in such a way as to prevent it from being turned town.

What's remarkable about Goddard's story is that he persisted even after being told no by the Air Force. And most people would give up at that point. But he kept trying different strategies until one succeeded, and he probably would never have come up with the idea for a documentary if he had given up on the idea altogether. Goddard's persistence kept him focused on strategies that could get him into the cockpit of a jet fighter.

Persistence isn't about knocking on the same brick wall until it falls down; it's about looking for weaknesses in the wall, digging under it, or finding a ladder to climb over it. When you persist in this fashion you look at failure not as an end point, but rather a feedback mechanism that shows you how to overcome your obstacle.

The power of persistence is knowing how to turn failure into inspiration.

Action: **Devise a reward plan for yourself.**

Programs like AA or Weight Watchers reward members for simply showing up and working the program. Their premise is regardless of failures or setbacks, persistence is necessary for progress to become possible.

Even the smallest of efforts deserve a reward. So this exercise is for you to find ways to reward yourself for your perseverance by setting tangible goals.

For example:

- Write a certain number of words.
- Exercise a certain length of time.
- Make a certain number of sales calls.
- Save a certain amount of money towards a trip or a purchase.
- Set rewards for meeting the goals (money, indulgences, treats, etc.).

Every time you reach one of these mini-goals, reward yourself with a treat, a movie you've wanted to see, a book you've wanted to buy, a call with a friend, or whatever little indulgence you consider to be a reward. You need to find ways to pat yourself on the back for a job well done.

Lesson 18

CREATE A WIN-WIN SITUATION

When Goddard filmed "Blackout in the Blue" it wasn't just a lesson in persistence, but a lesson in making a win-win situation out of a possible losing proposition.

Goddard's television producer had asked him if they could charge the Air Force $25,000 to film the documentary. He replied that in his original plan the documentary would be done at his expense since it was his dream that was going to be fulfilled. But John's producer insisted that $25,000 would be as much as they'd spend on one mission's worth of fuel. After all, the resulting training documentary helped the Air Force tremendously, so they had gained a great deal from Goddard's efforts.

Goddard still refused, saying he had made the deal on a handshake and wasn't about to go back on his word. To him he gained something very valuable from the experience: Three weeks of memories he would cherish forever, helping the Air Force, and getting to fly in one of their planes is how Goddard created a win-win situation.

Knowing that the once-in-a-lifetime experience of piloting a jet plane would be invaluable, he didn't need to receive a fee for his efforts. Instead, he earned it tenfold by putting the filmmaking on his resume so it would be impossible to forget.

In life we too often think about what's in it for us, and forget how powerful it can be to look at things in terms of a win-win situation. For example, an unpaid internship is still a win-win because it counts as experience the intern can put on their resume.

It's also important to create a win-win for the other side. The Air Force didn't have to pay Goddard for producing the documentary, which meant they risked very little by allowing him to produce it. Ultimately, the production was a win-win for both sides.

Find ways for everyone to win, and you're bound to see things in terms of the opportunities they present rather than the money you may have gotten paid (as you'll get rewarded in many different ways). Wherever there is an opportunity, your life will become richer and more fulfilling.

Action: **Look for ways to contribute to something that will provide valuable exposure, training, experience or inspiration.**

For this exercise you'll be searching for opportunities that will advance your goals and benefit another person or group of people.

For example:

- A person who wants to travel internationally may find that volunteering with a charity or mission group may result in a free or low-cost trip to an exotic part of the world.

- An artist who wants to sell their work may find they can get valuable exposure by contributing a piece of art to a charity drive.

- A biker who wants to train with professional bikers may get valuable experience from volunteering to be part of the Tour-de-France support team.

- An entrepreneur who wishes to break into a market may gain significant exposure if they offer to speak at conferences or volunteer at trade shows.

By thinking of opportunities in this light, you can find a whole new realm of possibilities to explore.

Lesson 19

BEGIN WITH A PLAN

Dwight Eisenhower once said that plans aren't important, but that planning is everything. It's through the act of planning where dreams and fantasies begin to be carved into reality. It is in planning where questions are asked, such as "If I want to achieve X, what must I do first?"

Which is why every adventure begins with a plan. Goddard demonstrated this by creating his life list full of adventures and goals. He didn't go into details about the plans, but it was the first step toward creating the plans.

In science you begin with a hypothesis, so when it comes to having an adventure you first have to have a goal. The goal is the first part of your plan, and then you work backwards from there to find out what's required to achieve that goal. How can you close the gap between where you are in life and what it would take to ultimately achieve that goal?

The process of getting from here to there – and everything in between – is the plan.

It doesn't matter if you're not very good at creating plans. For example, you don't have to be an expert on book publishing to get your novel published. Or you don't have to be a personal trainer to craft a plan to lose 50 pounds. You just have to be open to learning about what goes into a plan and how to find ways to make it happen.

A good plan needs to be two things:

1. **Actionable:** Your plan should include an action, something specific you can get started on right away. If your goal is to run a five-minute mile you could start running a mile every day until you can do it in five minutes.

2. **Flexible:** Your plan should be flexible so that you can alter it as you learn new information. It's not a lack of discipline or focus to change your plans as they're being developed because they're a work in progress. Your research and talking with other people will help it take shape. Eisenhower basically said that once you have a plan that meets these two criteria, you're ready to get to work. It's that simple!

Action: **Make an action plan that requires you to think through the details of accomplishing your goal.**

Your plan needs to be written down, so don't try to avoid this step. The strategy of writing down your goals is a main message from Goddard's life list that shows how much influence a piece of paper can have on the way you live.

This exercise is to plan out how you'll pursue and achieve one of the most inspiring and exciting goals on your life list. Get specific by including where and how you'll train, buy supplies, find resources, and overcome obstacles.

Document real expenses; make actual reservations; and ask real people to commit to the plan along with you. Making these specific plans will move you closer to achieving your goals.

Lesson

STAY AWAY FROM THE HERD

In the animal kingdom it's advantageous to travel in herds as there's safety, protection, and the advantage that if you come across prey you'll be able to outnumber them. If you've ever seen footage of a herd of gazelles in Africa being chased by a lion, you see them moving in unison. Because their main goal is flight and survival, they move as one for a common purpose.

However, in modern society a "herd" has a different connotation (if you've heard the term "herd mentality" you know exactly what this is referring to). In this context, the herd isn't a team like it is in nature, but rather a common attitude that keeps people from straying too far off the beaten path. It keeps the animals (sorry, people) together in a single focus that's solely for the purpose of the masses.

In society a herd is built on security and predictability: Get a stable job, find a stable mate, and live a stable life. In many cases the "herd" doesn't care how stable your life is; they just don't want you to rock their boat. They want to know they can wake up every morning and have life be the same day after day after boring day.

So to achieve your life's dreams it will require some separation from the "herd." You'll need to be prepared to rock the boat, because the very act of setting ambitious goals means you're going to step out of the box (the boat) and into some unstable waters.

When you come from a herd (friends, family, colleagues, peers) that isn't used to setting ambitious, unusual goals, they're going to be disturbed when they see you doing exactly that. They're going to feel unstable because one of the members of the herd has shaken their safe, secure existence and made them feel insecure and unsafe.

Most people wouldn't admit it, but they really don't want to be a part of a herd any more than you do. People who have lived their entire life in the herd have an unwavering set of attitudes and beliefs that aren't conducive to progress or achievement. In fact it's just the opposite; they've learned to move with the herd by not rocking the boat.

John Goddard's key for achieving goals? Stay away from the herd and walk your own path! You'll fine-tune your beliefs to align with your goals, not your environment or the mentality of those around you.

Staying out of the herd will help you to avoid the pitfalls and self-doubts that many suffer from. You'll find it easier to pursue your dreams if you stay away from the herd, and set a new standard for yourself: Achieving the dreams you've written down, and following the path you're blazing.

Action: **Initiate contact with someone who inspires you and who you think is out of your league.**

By this time you should be surrounding yourself with people who share your passions, and limiting contact with people who hold you back. However, as you've probably noticed, even people who inspire you at first may turn out to be part of the herd mentality and will try to hold you back.

This exercise is once again asking you to reach out to someone who inspires you; but this time you'll also do the following:

- Examine your peers to determine if they are spurring you on to better things, or trying to hold you back based on their own agenda.
- Evaluate your mentor or accountability partner to determine if you need to make a change and find someone more supportive.

Sometimes we bring people into our support sphere early in a growth stage, but find that as we progress they no longer fit our needs. That may sound mercenary, but growth brings in many changes and you need to be flexible and accept that people may fall by the wayside.

- Reach out to someone who inspires you that you think might be out of your league. You have elevated yourself to a whole new level of thinking, so people you chose to be around before may no longer fit with your aspirations. This is taking your relationships to a different level, because as they say… you want to surround yourself with the kind of people you want to become.

You don't want to be one of the herd running off the edge of the cliff to mediocrity. You want to be the trailblazer at the head of the herd setting the pace.

Lesson 21

ELIMINATE LIMITING SELF-TALK

There's a great deal of danger in being a member of the herd, but not because of the herd itself. Rather, it's the self-image you adopt when you view yourself as part of the herd and not as an individual.

John Goddard said the herd instinct is strongly engrained in people, and that there's a degree of comfort in being like everyone else. The problem is people who live this way often inflict a great deal of limiting self-talk upon themselves.

Limiting self-talk is what happens when you feel guilty, admonish yourself, or doubt yourself in your own thoughts. If you think you're stupid, clumsy or ugly, over time you begin to believe your own self-talk and you become what you think you are. This kind of self-deprecation is acceptable to the herd because it prevents you from venturing too far out on your own.

Over time your self-esteem degrades to a point of weakness. One day you wake up and realize that being a member of the herd isn't all it's cracked up to be.

The way to break out of the herd mentality is to change negative self-talk into positive pep-talk. Instead of blaming yourself for everything that goes wrong, you learn to be positive about what you're doing.

By saying, "I did a great job today!" you challenge your old doubts and replace them with new beliefs in your abilities and your goals. "I was really good at that speech," or "I look really pretty today," are positive affirmations that build the spirit instead of destroying it.

Self-talk is only as real as you accept it to be. If you have limiting beliefs like "I could never write a children's book," eventually the actions (or non-actions) you take reflect those beliefs. All you need to do is to change your negative self-belief into positive affirmations, and the results you want will follow.

You should also replace limiting self-talk with self-love. This isn't to say you should cross over into arrogance, but that you should truly love yourself the way you might love a family member, a close friend, and even a mate.

Think about this: If someone were to insult your parents or a loved one, would you stand idly by and allow the insults to fly? Or would you defend them saying "No! I have the greatest parents in the world. They are brilliant, loving, nurturing and are my best friends. It's *you* who has the problem!"

Similarly, you shouldn't let your mind toss insults at you. The next time you're aware of your limiting self-talk, stop yourself and say "No! I'm a great person and I have unlimited potential. I'm brilliant, loving, nurturing, and I'm my best friend!" Eventually, this self-respect will carry over to other aspects of your life and enrich it for the better.

Action: **Write down one thing you did right, and read it out loud before you go to bed and before you start the next day.**

Narrate your positive daily experiences to position yourself for success and to avoid discouragement. One of the most effective ways to do this is to establish the habit of writing down one thing you did right that day just before going to bed:

- Take time writing out the details of your accomplishment by asking yourself what made you feel good about yourself.

- After you've written down your accomplishment, allow yourself to feel proud of your actions.

- Then when you wake up the next morning, re-read it before you start your day (which instills a feeling of accomplishment, which establishes a mindset that you can do even more).

The added benefit is that you'll see the list of things you've done right grow by leaps and bounds, which will help you realize that yes, you are brilliant, nurturing, loving, supportive, intelligent, talented and creative. Or it will help point out one particular trait you can utilize to help you reach your goal.

Whatever the case may be, giving yourself a pat on the back for something you accomplished during the day is like giving a big hug to yourself for a job well done.

Lesson 22

PROVE YOURSELF

When John Goddard was ten years old he worked on his uncle's cattle ranch – a real, honest-to-goodness working ranch where real cowboys lived real cowboy lives. Initially, he was considered a greenhorn from California who got the work simply because he knew his uncle.

The cowboys expected the young boy to lollygag and be a nuisance, but rather than live up (or down, depending on which way you look at it) to their expectations, Goddard decided to prove them wrong and took it as a challenge. So he set about working hard six days a week from dawn until dusk right along with the men.

When his uncle told him, "John, you did pretty well today. I'm going to equal your pay to the ranch hands," he never felt more gratified or proud. He was doing real cowboy work and would be getting real cowboy pay. Better yet, he proved to the wranglers that he wasn't just some greenhorn from California, but someone worthy of working alongside them doing very hard cowboy work.

The best lesson Goddard took from the experience wasn't that he had proved the cowboys wrong. It was that he had proved himself to be valuable to them, to himself, and to his uncle.

Proving yourself to be worthy can be a daunting task. In Goddard's case it required tough work mending fences, digging irrigation canals, herding and branding. But in the end it was all worth it because of the admiration he received.

When you prove your self-worth you dismiss all the negative self-talk that says "you can't do this," and you'll discover a new confidence you never knew you had.

During your life you've had many opportunities to prove yourself. Maybe you went out for varsity basketball as a sophomore in high school and felt out of place. Or maybe you interviewed for a job and felt incompetent and unqualified. Maybe you picked up a phone to ask someone out on a date, but laid it back down because they had a different social status that you felt was much higher than yours.

So first and foremost, no matter who doubts you – your friends, your family, your coworkers, or even yourself – you need to prove that voice is wrong… wrong… WRONG!

Nothing will be more gratifying than when you prove yourself equal to a task. Yes, it's nice to show others that you can do it. But ultimately you do it to prove it to yourself.

Action: **Set a milestone goal that will be difficult to meet, and then crush that goal!**

As you've been working towards achieving your life goals, you've probably noticed some character flaws (or what you perceive to be flaws). Perhaps you're not as disciplined as you'd like to be, or you don't push yourself as hard as you know you can.

This exercise is to choose a tangible milestone of something you've never done before, and commit to reaching this goal. Let someone know about the goal you've set, and ask them to help keep you accountable.

Some possible milestone goals might be:

- Performing a specific number of repetitions, or lifting weights at a more challenging level

- Making an intimidating sales call

- Applying for a daunting job

- Selling yourself to a prospective buyer or client

- Writing a record number of pages for your screenplay
- Working more hours so you'll have the money set aside (and vacation time) for a long-awaited trip

Therefore, this entire lesson is about hard work and sheer determination. You need to put in the blood, sweat, and tears necessary to prove to yourself that you're strong enough to accomplish your goals.

Lesson 23

AVOID PROCRASTINATION

Hopefully you won't put off reading this lesson until tomorrow. Did I get your attention?

The great illusion of procrastination is believing the work you put off today will be easier to accomplish tomorrow. When you think, *I can finish this later,* you've given yourself permission to procrastinate like Scarlett O'Hara in *Gone With the Wind,* when she said, "After all… tomorrow is another day."

The reality is when tomorrow comes the work is still there, it will be just as hard, and you'll be a day further behind. Therefore, the more you procrastinate, the more the work piles up which makes it harder rather than easier to achieve success.

So the best way to handle procrastination is to learn better time management.

John Goddard carefully safeguarded his time. For example, when friends asked to come over to view his collection of artifacts, instead of putting off the work he had to do he protected his time by saying, "Could we do this next week? I've got a project I need to get done." This way his friends and his work had equal importance, and both things would get accomplished. A win-win all around.

If you get into the habit of procrastinating on little things – like exams, paying bills, sending out resumes, writing the first ten pages of your novel – you'll create a mindset that affects bigger things like your dreams and goals, which is where you'll really get yourself into trouble.

Action: **Create a mantra and a totem.**

The only way to avoid procrastination is to refuse to give in to it (in other words, quit procrastinating about procrastination!)

For this lesson you'll establish a simple mantra of one word: **NOW!** Write the word NOW! on sticky notes and place them all around your home and work space.

For the totem (an object used to test if one's self is in one's own reality): Make yourself a bracelet from beads that spell out the word NOW!, or get a stone carved with the word NOW! on it, or paint a small item with the word NOW! on it.

Keep this item in your pocket or on your desktop to remind you that you'll no longer allow yourself to procrastinate and waste time. No posting on Facebook. No more games on your iPad. No more surfing the Web or flipping through television channels. The totem is an in-your-face reminder that you'll get to work NOW!, and as a result you'll start seeing results NOW!

Lesson 24

AVOID WHERE ANGELS FEAR TO TREAD

Alexander Pope once wrote "Fools rush in where angels fear to tread." In essence he was saying that when wise people see that a situation is dangerous they stay away from it, whereas foolish people tend to forge ahead in spite of the danger.

When combined with the lesson on herd mentality, you can see that many people don't have a very good idea of what is considered dangerous, so collectively they go right over the cliff to their demise. After all, if the leader of the herd thinks it's okay, then it must be safe. Right? Well …

Consider where "fools rush in" in today's society. Where is the most competition? For example, standard jobs in the marketplace have a great deal of competition, whereas you would face less competition if you were to create your own job and your own niche.

Avoiding the herd mentality means you're going to follow the wise angels that know when it's dangerous to tread, and not the fools who are clueless. In Lesson 2 you learned about thinking outside the box, which is precisely what "avoiding where angels fear to tread" means.

This may seem contradictory, but let me explain further.

John Goddard put himself in a lot of dangerous situations throughout his life, which means an angel might have feared to tread in his footsteps. But consider the risks Goddard might not have taken if he had chosen a more conservative path. He didn't want to end up like those adults in his parents' living room saying, "I wish I could be John's age again." To him that was more dangerous than any risk he could take in the wilds of Africa.

Which is why it's important not to take heed of every bit of conventional wisdom about danger, or follow the herd mentality. When someone tries to explain that what you're doing is wrong, don't automatically take their word for it. What may seem dangerous to them may not be to you if it's a goal you want to pursue. If fools rush in where angels fear to tread, then maybe conventional wisdom isn't as wise as it's made out to be.

You need to follow your own heart and listen to your own dreams. You'll accomplish far more when you blaze your own path because you're your only competition. You've made the decision to tread where angels won't, and in that bit of "foolishness" there is wisdom because you did it on your own terms.

Of course you need to be prudent about a dangerous situation and take precautionary measures to protect yourself. Being daring doesn't always mean you have to put yourself in harm's way, so it makes sense to find ways to safely walk the path to success and leave yourself open to possibilities.

Action: **Brainstorm new and improved routes to success.**

You may find roadblocks as you pursue your goals. Maybe you can't get a talent agent to promote your music or acting career, or perhaps you haven't been able to get a new job.

It's possible your mentor has encouraged you to risk too much in investments or business ventures, and you're afraid you're going to get burned. If you've been hitting obstacles, you might feel like doing something desperate or giving up altogether.

This exercise is to brainstorm for safe alternate routes to success. For example:

- Writers can self-publish and self-promote online.

- Artists or inventors can partner with techies to get a portfolio or product online.
- Moonlighting can provide experience as you build a freelance portfolio.
- An older athlete can serve as a mentor if your current trainer is too young, too tough, or out of touch with your physical limitations.

Look for routes to success that will be safe and trustworthy without compromising your goals or diverting you from success.

Lesson 25

HAVE A "SOUL GOAL"

Having a "soul goal" means having a goal so important that it meets your needs at the core of your soul. It goes beyond money, fame, or glory – since all those things are superficial – and touches you on a purely emotional and often spiritual level.

You only get one life to live and you're in it. If you're not making goals so close to your heart that they inspire passion just by thinking about them, then it may be time to give thought to what a "soul goal" means to you. It's important to set the right goals from the very outset, so if you don't think about what's truly important you may have to revise your plans.

For many people a soul goal is something they think about all the time, and they don't have to ask themselves what their number one goal in life is. For others a soul goal is a little more difficult to determine.

Have you ever talked about the importance of setting goals with someone only to have them complain they don't know what they want out of life? It's not a pleasant situation for either of you to be in.

Not having a goal can make you feel lonely and lost, and the world around you can seem vague and mysterious. Instead of feeling inspired for getting up in the morning, you want to hide under the covers and hope it all goes away. Which is why it's very important for you to take the time to figure out what you truly want from your life.

And you can do this by asking yourself some important questions. For example, if you're sitting on your deathbed and looking back on your life, what one success would you want to stand out amongst all the others? What would break your heart if you didn't see one particular goal come to fruition?

Don't think about all the different things you want to accomplish; instead, focus on *the one* that will make you feel good about how you lived your life.

Action: **Focus only on actions that feed your soul. Take a break from activities that feel like work or you feel pressured to perform. Let your soul breathe.**

Instead of focusing on money, fame, or the hard work involved in accomplishing your life list, focus on the heart of your pursuits. Ask yourself what can you pursue that will feed your soul? Then commit to feeding your soul unconditionally and with purpose.

For example:

- If you're an artist, you might contribute artwork for a charity fundraiser, and ask that profits from the sale be given to a particular family in need or shelter.

- If you're an athlete, you could mentor a special needs child or youth-at-risk.

- If you're a small business owner, you could take on an intern who needs experience and inspiration.

Sometimes feeding your soul means pursuing a goal simply because you like how it feels. So you may wish to do something like the following:

- If you're an athlete, you may wish to slow down and enjoy your workout, and exercise at a level that nourishes your sense of well-being instead of pushing yourself too hard.

- Perhaps you'd benefit from taking a week off from exercising altogether, and indulging in massage or reflexology sessions to allow your body to heal so you can perform well when you start to exercise again.

- If you're an artist, you may wish to spend the week working on a piece simply for the joy of it. Create something that feels like pure artistic expression with no thoughts of selling or commercializing the piece.

- If you're a business owner, you may wish to take a week to focus solely on innovation or motivation instead of growing the business or marketing.

Whatever you do for this exercise, set aside the pressure to perform. Listen to your soul and let it guide you toward your accomplishments.

Lesson 26

COMMIT TO NATURE

John Goddard obviously was heavily immersed in nature. From a young age he was fascinated with nature's extremes like wide winding rivers, tall mountains, and thick jungles. In his life list he made sure to include an abundance of nature, because for him becoming immersed in an adventure was as close to true living as any man could hope for.

Committing to nature is important in several ways. Experiencing the outdoors in an exploratory, adventurous spirit helps you reconnect with your primordial instincts. Simply put, human beings were meant to be outside, even if it doesn't always feel that way.

It's also important to commit to nature, because if you're to truly live a rich life you have to fill it with a variety of unique experiences. Yes, routine and habit both have their places. But getting out in nature and exploring the unexplored provides experiences on which to build an entire lifetime's worth of stories and memories.

Communing with nature was how John Goddard acquired most of his stories. But it wasn't just the physical aspects of nature he enjoyed; it was also the social experimentation that took place every time he came in contact with local natives.

By exposing himself to new cultures, Goddard was able to experience a richness of humanity and societal structure that most people don't even care to read about, much less go out and explore on their own.

Of course, you don't have to travel to the Congo or the Amazon to commune with nature. Instead, you can enjoy everything nature has to offer all around you. Every day you're exposed to a sunrise and a sunset, so why not experience them more often? If you live in the country, you could take time to look at the stars and learn about the constellations. Or find out more about the wildlife and birds in your area.

Maybe there's an arboretum, apiary (just take your bee sting kit along), aviary (unless the movie "The Birds" frightened you), or a butterfly sanctuary in your area (we won't even mention "Silence of the Lambs"). I'm just having a bit of fun with you, but you can see that there are all sorts of ways to get out of the house and take time to enjoy everything that Mother Nature tends for you.

Hiking, fishing, hunting, swimming, walking are all activities you can undertake when you commit to nature. Not only will they help you get fresh air and exercise, but they'll help you reconnect with what's truly important in your life. It's hard not to reflect on your life list with more accuracy when you're out in nature.

So take advantage of where you live. Go out and experience the earth the way it is meant to be experienced, because your time here isn't as vast as you might think.

Action: **Get out into nature every day.**

Many of your life goals may require hard work and time inside, but you'll want to include enjoyment of nature on your life list.

This exercise is about committing to discovering or rediscovering nature in your daily life. Some suggestions include:

- Watch a sunrise or sunset for a full five minutes.
- Take a hike at a local trail or park.
- Stop to smell a flower, crunch a leaf underfoot, make a snowball, or feel the sun on your face.

- Bring your laptop outside and work on your patio, or at an outside table at work or a coffee shop.
- Listen to a babbling brook, or watch the beauty of a water fountain.

Reconnecting with nature is available to you in hundreds of ways. You just have to open your mind to allow it in (or back in) to your life.

Lesson 27

WRITE IT DOWN

Another powerful lesson to take from John Goddard's life is also one of the simplest:

If you have a goal, write it down ("build it – they will come!").

John Goddard's life list is what made him so famous. From a very young age he realized an important truth that many other successful people have realized: That writing down your aspirations helps make them more real and tangible.

Emmitt Smith, the famous football star, said during his Hall of Fame speech, "It's only a dream until you write it down – then it becomes a goal." Smith wrote down many of his goals, including becoming the Super Bowl MVP and becoming the NFL's all-time leading rusher. He accomplished both and checked them off his list.

You can discover the power of writing down your dreams and aspirations this very moment. But before you write them down, it's important to consider what's truly important to you. What are you so passionate about that once you commit to it you'll follow through on your goals without hesitation? What important achievement could change your life and leave you with a sense of fulfillment and pride?

Once you have your answer, you're ready to write down your aspirations. And in doing so, they can be transformed from mere daydreams to real-life goals.

John Goddard's goals were specific and outcome-oriented; so you need to be very specific about your goals. Don't say you want to become a famous singer which is too vague. Think instead how you'd define "famous." Writing down that you want to sing at Carnegie Hall, the New York Metropolitan Opera, or the Grand Ole Opry is a goal you can check off one day because you'll know when it's accomplished.

Or you can write down that you want to go white water rafting down the Snake River, climb Mt. Rainier, go down the trail to the bottom of the Grand Canyon, or write a book about a specific topic.

It's also important to focus on what action you'll take after you write down your goal. If your goal is to run a five-minute mile, you could take up the habit of running one mile per day. If your goal is to sing at the Met, you can take singing lessons. If you want to raft down a river take rafting lessons, do research online, or get brochures about programs available.

Your plan doesn't have to be overly complicated or detailed; it just has to be written down so you can start breaking your goal into attainable components to take you step-by-step closer towards your goal.

Action: **Write a contract to yourself promising you'll focus on your goals.**

This exercise is about writing your goals in a contract to yourself, and making it official by signing it, framing it, and placing it where you can see it regularly.

It's time to supercharge your dreams, and remind yourself daily about the actions you need to be taking.

It's time to revisit your life list to see what progress you've made. Go through your list to check off goals you've accomplished, and choose a new goal or set of goals to focus on (even if you haven't checked any off at this point).

If you aren't ready to move on to new goals, recommit to the goal(s) you chose at the beginning of this program. Write down the details and the accompanying plans that will make the goal become a reality.

Lesson

GIVE YOUR GOALS A DEADLINE

Lesson 23 showed you how bad procrastination can be for your goals. Procrastination is the lie we tell ourselves that tomorrow will be easier than today, when in reality tomorrow is just the same as today – it's just 24 hours later.

If you want to achieve your goals you'll have to beat procrastination, which means setting deadlines. Rather than hoping your goal is achieved one day, you set a concrete date as a guide for crafting a plan for achieving your goal. "I need to have a plan in place for achieving this goal, because I need to have it done by New Year's Eve (or whatever the goal date is)."

If you have a goal of running a five-minute mile and then run a mile each day to train for it, that's great. But if you add a deadline to that training, you can measure your progress. For instance, if you know you're on week 5 of 21 allotted weeks of training, then you know how close you are to your goal. Having a measurable deadline allows you to track your progress and make adjustments as needed.

You might ask, "If I set a deadline for my goals, how long should I give myself?" which is a tricky question to answer. On one hand, you don't want to wait too long when you can achieve your goals sooner than you think. On the other hand, you don't want to press too hard and burn out, and then feel like a failure because you didn't reach an unrealistic deadline you set for yourself.

So you need to determine what a realistic deadline means to you.

Evaluate where you are now, and figure out how long it should take you to achieve the goal. Using our five-minute mile example, you could first run one mile to establish how long it takes so you can set a realistic length of time to run one in five minutes.

Then take that deadline and give it a nudge towards being a little bit more challenging. You want a goal that excites you, because the deadline will roll around sooner than later. This also pushes you to achieve more than you originally thought yourself capable of doing.

Action: **Create a milestone plan for your goals.**

Take out the contract you wrote in Lesson 27 and review it. Now write out a plan for your goals, including milestones and deadlines; then add those to your calendar.

Commit to scheduling necessary training, appointments and resources to make sure your plan is detailed and actionable.

Lesson

GIVE YOUR GOALS A BUDGET

When you plan a vacation you know your allocated time and your budget, so why not plan a goal the same way? After all, a vacation is simply an achievement of a goal even in its own small way.

But when it comes to budgeting your goal, you're going to be budgeting your time.

To stick with our earlier example, consider how much time you'd have to budget per day to run a five-minute mile. Chances are you have to add time for getting dressed, eating carbs (if that's what you do), stretching, getting to where you're going to run if it's not outside your front door, coming back home, and taking a shower. So you might have to budget as much as an hour per day to run.

Obviously, that means you'll have an hour less for other activities during your day, so this is where the "budgeting" comes into play. Just as you look for ways to save money during a vacation, you'd look at your daily routine to see if there are ways to fit your new activity within your time budget.

For example, is it better to run in the morning or after work? Is there time during your lunch break where you can squeeze in your training? What would be required of you if you did squeeze that time in (i.e., would you have to bring a gym bag to work, and where would you clean up after running)?

Your goals don't happen in the dream world – they happen in real life, which means you're going to have to sacrifice time and effort towards your goal's achievement.

So you need to establish a budget. Whether that means saving money to spend on your goal or finding more time, some degree of budgetary sacrifice will have to be made. If you make this sacrifice an integral part of your plan from the very beginning, the entire road toward your goal is sure to be smoother.

Action: **Establish a time and/or money budget.**

This exercise is to get you to invest money and time to make your dreams happen. Buy necessary supplies; pay for a mentor, trainer or coach; or programs that give you tools to attain your goal. Figure out what you'll need to cut from your existing time and money budgets to make room for your passion.

Then fill in the time investment on your calendar. Start by scheduling time devoted to pursuing your dreams just as you would schedule a doctor's appointment or a coffee date.

If your goal includes doing something on a regular basis, fill that slot with that commitment to prevent you from filling it with another activity. This way you're still within budget and on your way to your goal!

Lesson

WHAT YOU RESIST PERSISTS

On the surface an assertion like "what you resist persists" doesn't make a lot of sense. Logically, if you resist something won't it eventually go away? In reality, the more you resist circumstances, attitudes or even people, the more those things seem to have power over you.

Which brings us to an old success principle: Energy goes where you focus your attention. If you focus on good things, you tend to get more good things. If you focus on bad stuff – even if your focus is simply "I don't want this to happen!" – you tend to get more bad stuff.

What you resist persists because it has to do with where your focus lies. If you set goals like John Goddard did, but your next step was to think about all the obstacles you'd have to overcome, then guess what? Those obstacles are going to become overwhelming and loom bigger than they should. Eventually, they'll seem so large that you won't believe it's worth pursuing the goal you set for yourself. But if you focus instead on what you can do to achieve your goal and how to circumvent any obstacles, you'll have much better results.

Let's say your goal comes right out of the John Goddard playbook, and that you want to build your own telescope (a goal he achieved). If you focus on the fact you know nothing about telescopes, you won't be spending your time budget learning how to build a telescope. Focusing on the obstacles in essence becomes an obstacle.

In football, coaches tell their quarterbacks that even though 6'5" defensive ends are chasing them, it's important to keep their eyes down the field to find the wide receivers. If the quarterback is only concerned about the pass rush, they'll fail to see the potential touchdown throw because they're so busy looking at who's going to tackle them!

So you need to keep your eyes down the field. Don't resist the obstacles – run right by them and get a touchdown!

Action: **Write a three to five-word mantra.**

One of the most effective ways to increase focus is through meditation that will relax and energize you, and help you become laser-focused on your goal.

This exercise is to come up with a very short three to five-word mantra that embodies your intended focus. You'll spend five minutes each day repeating this mantra as you breathe in and breathe out while meditating on your area of focus.

You can choose a mantra such as:

- "I always win."
- "No mountain is too high."
- "I ace the interview."
- "I am a runner."
- "I am daring and adventurous."
- "I achieve my goals."
- "I am a winner."
- "I can do this and I know I can." (Okay, that's a little more than five words, but it has been one of my favorites!)

Whatever it is, make it present tense (I am) instead of future tense (I will), and an affirmative action.

Set a timer for five minutes. Clear everything from your mind, and during those five minutes repeat your mantra with each inhalation and exhalation. Focus only on your breathing and the repetition of your mantra.

Setting aside five minutes (your "five-minute mental mile") to become hyper-focused on your goal will help visualize it into reality (and doing it first thing in the morning can make you feel calm and centered throughout the rest of your day).

Lesson 31

MENTALLY REHEARSE THE OUTCOME

You'd rehearse before performing in a play, or playing in a piano recital. So why not rehearse your goal outcomes?

John Goddard was an avid believer in the power of visualization. In fact, he tells the story of coming upon an impossible cataract on the Nile (an area full of whirlpools, rocks, and obstacles). So rather than braving the treacherous river and hoping for the best, he walked along the banks, visualizing what he'd need to do to get his kayak through the obstacles.

When it was time to navigate the rapids Goddard half-closed his eyes, followed his mentally-rehearsed course, and made it through the cataract without any problems. According to Goddard he had imagined every step perfectly, and didn't break one paddle.

You too can utilize the power of visualization to mentally rehearse outcomes. Do you want to nail that job interview? Then come up with a list of the most common questions interviewers ask and rehearse your answers. When it's time to go to the interview you can relax knowing you've already practiced the scenario in your mind. You'll come across as confident, calm, self-assured and the person they need to hire.

Not only does mentally rehearsing help you be prepared for what comes next, it gives you a boost in confidence. The more accurately and vividly you rehearse your outcomes the more you'll feel prepared, which will help you to perform better when the time comes.

You can mentally rehearse anything. For example, before sitting down to write a chapter of your novel, spend a few moments picturing yourself in a state of flow with the words pouring out of you. If you have to meet your significant other's parents for the first time, mentally rehearse it going well and everybody getting along. Picture yourself interacting with them without feeling nervous.

You'll be amazed at what mental rehearsal can do for you, particularly if you've never tried it before. Take a few minutes and rehearse the most important upcoming events in your life, which just might make the difference between success and failure.

Action: **Prepare a narration of how you see the event.**

Now that you've begun your venture into meditation as a motivational tool, you'll want to extend the practice to mentally visualizing your success which needs to be a structured effort in order for it to be effective.

You first need to identify an obstacle or tricky part of your goal (perhaps something that intimidates you, or makes you doubt you can perform up to par). Now outline the steps you'll need to take to succeed, and write them on an index card.

Record yourself slowly reading the steps out loud, allowing time to lapse between each step until you've recorded your entire plan of action. Repeat the plan step-by-step until you have five full minutes of recording.

Then use the recording during your morning meditation routine. Set a timer for five minutes. Close your eyes and listen to your narration of the steps you must follow to succeed. Concentrate on your breathing, your narration, and a mental image of you following those steps carefully and confidently to success.

Lesson 32

PROGRAM YOUR SUBCONSCIOUS

It's not always easy to spot when your subconscious is at work, since throughout the day you have many thoughts that shape your attitudes and beliefs. But if you want more success, you're going to have to learn how to "program" this part of your psyche so that it works for you instead of against you.

Have you ever talked to someone who seemed dead set on not taking any action toward their goals? Even though you've tried to convince them how easy it would be to get started, they seemed to have an excuse for everything you say. Well, this is the kind of person whose subconscious is getting in the way of their success. Their negative programming is so strong they can't grasp the very notion of success.

John Goddard remarked that he often encountered people who seemed to suffer from a negative subconscious. Apparently one of his friends who suffered a similar form of cancer as Goddard didn't fare as well with the treatment because he expected the cancer to kill him.

Goddard took a different approach to his own treatment, believing he should continue working and getting on with his life. In doing so, he cultivated a subconscious expectation of beating the cancer (which he did for many years until he succumbed to a rare form called Waldenström's Macroglobulinemia). The point here being that he had reprogrammed his subconscious so he could continue his adventures, and lived a very long life in spite of his disease.

In order to make sure things go your way, you have to program your subconscious into a certain mindset, and there are several ways to accomplish this:

Affirmations: Affirmations are more than simply repeating a positive sentence; they can be incantations through which you cultivate positive emotions and the expectation of success.

Visualization: There are many studies that show the subconscious doesn't discern between imagined and real experiences. Therefore, using imagined experiences will build your confidence and positive attitude.

Master your emotions: Surround yourself with positive emotions, because as you get "addicted" to the positivity you'll come to expect positive things out of life. And the more you enjoy life, the more you'll learn it's not to be avoided but to be embraced.

Action: **Listen to your five-minute narration as you go to sleep each night.**

Incorporate all three elements (affirmations, visualization, mastering your emotions) for at least a few minutes per day, and you'll notice a subtle but powerful shift in your subconscious expectations which will reshape your reality.

Now that you've learned morning visualization meditative techniques, we're going to switch things up a bit. Instead of meditating each morning, in this exercise you're going to listen to your narration each night when you go to bed, and fall asleep to the sound of your own voice.

You've already done the heavy lifting of concentrated visualization. Now you can simply listen to your voice telling you what you need to do to succeed, and trust your subconscious to work on the issues as you sleep.

Lesson 33

DO YOUR HOMEWORK

This one single lesson can give you an advantage over 99% of people.

For many people "homework" is something they'd do at school. The truth is, many people lack knowledge on how to do basic preparations that could really improve various aspects of their lives. Homework, due diligence, preparation, research – whatever you want to call it – they don't do it, so they often go into a situation severely unprepared.

Goddard's habit of visualizing and mentally rehearsing the steps of his adventures could be considered a form of mental "homework." But there are other ways to do homework that can give you a game-changing advantage.

For example: how much homework do you do before a job interview? Do you review your resume in order to remember your positions and responsibilities, then expect to walk in and ace it?

Or do you do your due diligence and become well-armed with information before meeting your potential employer? For instance, you could research the ten most frequently asked questions, prepare your answers, learn more about the company you're interviewing with, and prepare questions to ask them as you need to know if the company is a right fit for you.

Some football coaches like to say games are won on the practice field and not on game day. This is often the case in real life, because your preparation is where you find the advantages. If you can out-prepare your competition, you can end up beating them.

Gale Sayers, a star NFL running back, said he worked so hard during off-season that by the time training camp rolled around the physical efforts were easy. This is the kind of "off-season homework" you should be doing when it comes to your performance.

If you're faced with an executive meeting, running a five-minute mile, climbing a mountain, or giving a speech, you should be so well-prepared that the event becomes less of a challenge than you thought it would be.

Many people save hundreds of dollars per grocery shopping trip simply because they do their homework: Knowing which stores to shop, what days during the week have the best deals, what kind of holiday offers are available, which coupons are available, etc. It's not the actual shopping that makes them so good at saving money – it's their homework and coupon clipping they do at home.

Doing homework for just about any challenge in your life will help you achieve a greater amount of success. And before you say that there isn't any homework to do in your field, there's always some form of preparation to be done. Always! So if you're a good student and do your homework, and are better prepared for success, you might just get an A!

Action: **Devote a set amount of time for research and for asking questions.**

We've taken some time off from action work to make sure you're still motivated and have programmed yourself mentally to keep working towards your goals.

Now it's time to do the work required to succeed through the following [suggested] exercises:

- Go online to find out as much as possible about the event or company.
- Go to a seminar (or attend a webinar) where you'll learn what it takes to accomplish your goals.

- Will you need special equipment?
- What's the best training program?
- What's the latest software, the most effective techniques, the most important survival tips to master?
- Who else has gone before you and achieved this challenge? If no one has, what were their obstacles? Why was it so out of range that they failed or didn't try?

Then adjust your plan, milestones and budget to accommodate your new information.

Lesson 34

GET OVER YOURSELF

Goddard had a lot of positive things to say about the 21st century. He loved how easy it was to travel compared to prior centuries, and how modern conveniences made the life he lived possible.

But even conveniences have their pitfalls. Social media and communication technology (i.e., Facebook, Twitter and Skype) have made the world smaller, which brings people together from around the world who otherwise would never have met. But there's also a lot of excessive attention-grabbing that isn't conducive to living a rich, well-rounded life.

In short, we all need to get over ourselves.

Many people think it's who they are that makes them special – materialism, notoriety, success (the old keeping up with the Joneses nonsense). But in reality what makes them special is what they do with their time.

For example, it's easy to go to bed every night telling yourself you'll start working toward your goal the next day. You have good intentions, even if you're not actively working toward achieving those goals, so you close your eyes and nod off feeling good about yourself.

The problem with that is intentions will get you nowhere, nor get you the accolades you're seeking. If you always intend on working out but never do, you won't get someone saying, "Hey, you look great!" What you do with that intention is what brings positive attention.

So you need to get over yourself and realize you're no different or more special than anyone else. No one's going to hand your goals to you on a silver platter – you've got to make them happen.

If you believe you have what it takes to be a famous author, but never send out your work to publishers, who's going to come knocking on your door on the off chance they'll find a great author behind it? Absolutely no one. How is the world going to find you if you don't make yourself visible to the world? It doesn't owe you anything simply because you want it.

Comedian and actor Steve Martin said, "Be so good they can't ignore you." This doesn't mean you become so arrogant you can't get your head through a door. The truth is you're a commodity, and you have to get yourself out into the world for it to notice you. You need to give the world something worthy of their attention.

Action: **Carve out two extra hours you'll devote to pursuing your goal.**

It's time to knuckle down and become so good the world can't ignore you. You learned in the previous lesson that homework is an invaluable step to preparing for every step along the way to your goal.

These two hours are nose-to-the-grindstone type of hard work. So this exercise is about carving extra time out of your schedule to develop your skills, or decide how you want the world to look at you.

Even John Goddard had a specific persona, skills, tools, and ways of circumventing obstacles to achieve his goals. He got over himself at age 15, and found ways to show the world that he was a great guy doing great deeds.

So carve out two extra hours you can devote exclusively to advancing your goal. Then decide what you should do that will give you the biggest bang for your buck in those two hours. Protect them like they are gold, and make sure nothing or no one gets in the way of your extra hard work.

Lesson 35

SEE THE BIG PICTURE

A lot of people can't see the forest because the trees are in their way.

"Think big" is advice given so often that it borders on becoming cliché, but there are reasons people still need to hear it. Why? Sadly, it's because they don't realize what they're capable of.

When John Goddard sat down and wrote his life list at age 15, it was a very ambitious set of goals. It included exploring all over the world, learning difficult skills, and taking on physical challenges. At that moment his full potential was realized for the rest of his life because he thought big and wanted to achieve big things.

Your full potential can be realized if you set your sights on bigger goals and then find ways to achieve those goals, rather than setting just okay goals and never challenging yourself to any significant degree. This is why it's very important to step back and look at the big picture (another example of visualization and mental rehearsing).

In Lesson 27 it was mentioned that Emmitt Smith wasn't even in the NFL before he set a goal of becoming the all-time leading rusher. Talk about seeing the big picture! While other football players were still thinking about high school or college, Smith saw himself rushing for records in the National Football League.

Seeing the big picture also means maintaining humility and appreciating what's truly important in life. It's often not the achievement of a goal that makes you a success, but rather what you had to go through in order to achieve that goal. The challenges you encounter ultimately define you rather than the achievement itself.

In order to achieve great things you're going to have to become a great person. Now, don't be frightened. This doesn't mean you have to be another Mahatma Gandhi or Mother Teresa or Leonardo da Vinci. It just means you need to become the best person you can be.

So seeing the big picture is acknowledging that the rough spots during your journey aren't in your way, but rather they **are the journey**. It's the challenges that will improve you the most and help you become a great person, whatever that ends up meaning to you.

Your big picture in life *is* a challenge. If achieving goals were easy, we'd all be gathered at a fire-walking ceremony in Bali. Instead, it takes passion and commitment to shape your life into what you want it to be.

Can you see the big picture well enough to know that a little temporary discomfort today will be worth achieving a goal tomorrow? If so, you have what it takes to succeed.

Action: **Make a storyboard of your big picture.**

In advertising or filmmaking a storyboard is an outline of the proposed project that contains a sequence of sketches depicting the progression of a project from beginning to end. This way the production teams have the big picture in their minds before going to press or committing to shooting schedules.

This exercise is about making a big picture storyboard for one of your most exciting and challenging life goals. It will show you how to see the entire big picture from inception to completion of your goal, and everything in between to make it happen.

On this storyboard you'll create a timeline that starts at the origination of your journey (think back to that very first day where you started taking steps toward your goal). It could be a day, a week, a month, a year – but you need to pinpoint where your journey toward your goal first started:

- On the timeline you'll add dates, notes, photos, clippings and memorabilia that will help you see what you've done thus far to pursue your goal.

- Once you get to what you're doing at this point in time, write down three things you've learned about yourself during your journey to get here.
- Then you'll think past today going forward on your journey. Add to your storyboard what needs to happen to accomplish your goal by using words, pictures and images you find online or in magazines.
- The last step is when you finally achieve your goal. What does it look like? Are you standing on top of Mt. Everest? Are you holding a blue ribbon for the best pie in the county? Are you holding a check for that screenplay or novel you've written?

Then step back, review your storyboard, and you'll see that it can – and will – become a reality.

Lesson 36

TAKE CARE OF YOUR BODY

How much do you think you can accomplish if you don't have the full cooperation of your body? If you're so out of shape that you can't get up a flight of stairs without breathing heavily, or you have such low energy you can't muster the enthusiasm to get out of bed, you need to fix what's wrong with your body.

No matter what your goals are, just about everything you do will need you to be in good shape. Taking care of your body requires a synergy of effort, and a mindset that you'll do what it takes to achieve your goal.

Synergy is a collaborative collection of efforts for the good of the whole. To help your body get strong and healthy – so you can climb those stairs or have energy to tackle the steps towards your goal – you need to incorporate these steps into your daily routine:

Physical exercise: Goddard made sure to include physical exercise goals as part of his life list, and as a result he was rewarded with a strong body that helped him achieve his goals.

Proper diet: There's a lot of conflicting information about what the best and worst foods are. But you know that junk food, food containing processed sugar, GMO processed elements (such as canola oil), and artery-clogging trans fats will be your downfall. At this point in your life you most likely know what is and isn't healthy. And with all the information available on the Internet there are no excuses not to develop a healthy diet for your body type and nutritional needs.

Sleep: A bad night's sleep affects your entire day. Committing more time to getting a good night's sleep every night will help you feel alert and energetic as opposed to lethargic and sluggish. During sleep your body heals and muscles repair, which gets you ready for the next day.

Entire books have been written on how to best take care of your body. But the truth is it takes commitment from you. Period.

Consider that 30 minutes of exercise is only 2% of your day, and 60 minutes is only 4% of your total day. Even if you subtract 8 hours of sleeping, an hour of exercise is still 6.25% of your time. Is your physical health worth the investment of only 6% or less of your time each day?

Committing to as little as 15 to 30 minutes per day toward your physical health will affect all areas of your life: How well you sleep, how well you concentrate, and how well you feel. If you invest in your body, your body will ultimately pay you dividends. So please make the investment since it's only a small fraction of your time.

Action: **Choose a healthy habit to pursue (or an unhealthy habit to quit) that will affect your overall health.**

This exercise is to evaluate your overall health and write down the areas you need to improve. Then choose one unhealthy habit to change and place this on your life list.

Some suggestions are:

- Get eight hours of sleep every night.
- Quit smoking.
- Limit or eliminate alcohol consumption.
- Eat a minimum of one helping of fresh, uncooked fruits and vegetables (preferably organic) every day.
- Take vitamins every day.
- Floss.

- Choose one food item from your diet you know is bad for you and eliminate it.

- Drink water, tea or coffee instead of soda or sweetened beverages.

Whatever healthy habit you choose to pursue, get it on your life list today. Choosing one is just a start so you aren't overwhelmed by trying to change everything all at once.

One step will get you closer toward your goal. Then you can start incorporating more changes to get your body as healthy as possible.

Lesson 37

COUNT YOUR BLESSINGS

Since John Goddard was an adventurer and explorer, a lot of people asked him if he would have preferred to live back in the 18th and 19th centuries when there were still plenty of undocumented and unchartered waters to explore.

He said he wouldn't go back to those times; that he was grateful to be living during more contemporary times of jets flying faster than bullets, and instant communication instead of having to wait weeks for mail. To Goddard, there was no better time to explore and seek adventure than the present.

But his attitude was part of a larger lesson: That it's important to count your blessings. Even when your circumstances are really bad – you're losing relationships, people in your life are dying, you have an illness, you encounter rejection – it's not an excuse to forget about all the things that are going right in your life. Goddard counted his friends and family as some of his major blessings, as well as the amazing times in which he lived.

No matter where you are in your life you have something to be thankful for, or the opportunity to create it. (Simply by reading these words you can be thankful for the gift of literacy – a gift that not everyone in the world gets to enjoy.) If you had breakfast and lunch today, you can be thankful for a full stomach. Heck, you can be thankful the sun rises and sets every single day.

Shifting to an attitude that focuses on the positive things in your life will help you not only see your circumstances in a better light, but will better prepare you for any obstacles that may lie ahead.

If you know you have a lot to be thankful for, you won't feel so desperate to get approval of others. When you think about happiness as a mindset, you'll see why gratitude is so important.

The happiest people in life aren't happy because things always go well for them. They're happy because they've committed to making happiness a habit. It's how they choose to feel when they get up in the morning, and how they choose to feel when they go to bed at night. They *choose* to be happy and to count their blessings for all the good things in their life.

Gratitude starts with appreciating what you already have. And when you add being committed to your goals, the sense of fulfillment will build toward something even greater.

No one will come up to you and give you permission to be happy and grateful – you have to do it yourself. So what are you grateful for today? What makes you happy? And what makes you want to count your blessings?

Action: **Think about something you're grateful for every day, and then verbalize your gratitude.**

This exercise is to think about positive things you're grateful for, and to verbally share your gratitude with one person every day this week. You can do this by...

- Mentioning something positive in passing such as "Isn't the weather great today?" "Wasn't that a gorgeous sunset?" "Man, I'm feeling great today!"

- Complimenting someone who has helped you or made your life more pleasant (this is a great pay-it-forward exercise as it helps them feel blessed about their life as well). "Isn't that a gorgeous necklace you're wearing?" "I'm so thrilled you have computer skills to help me load this software." "I couldn't have done this without you."

- Expressing gratitude for a service available to you.
- Sharing your good fortune with another person (again, paying it forward).
- Telling a friend or partner about something positive that happened that day.

Count your blessings out loud. If you can tie your positivity to a specific goal you're pursuing, then all the better.

Lesson

STAY SAFE BUT CURIOUS

Curiosity is one of the most important characteristics to have if you want to lead a rich life.

It's curiosity that drove some of the greatest minds to their discoveries. Sir Isaac Newton wouldn't have discovered the laws of gravity if he hadn't looked at an apple and the moon, and wondered if the same phenomenon kept both objects close to the earth.

In 2012, NASA's Voyager 1 probe crossed into interstellar space, becoming the first manmade object to exit the solar system. If it weren't for scientific curiosity, the Voyager would never have existed to explore the solar system.

Similarly, curiosity in your own life can drive you to achieve great things. Sometimes it works as an impetus to motivation. For example, if you're single and want to approach a member of the opposite sex, your curiosity about them provides the itch to do something about it. You want to see whether or not the risk will be worth the reward (or lack of).

Be curious about possibilities without worrying about the net results (which are often a complete surprise). Submit your novel to publishers. Try out for the varsity basketball team. Hold your first business meeting. There is safety in trying without worrying about net results. You can be hopeful, of course. But if you don't ask you don't get; if you don't try you can't succeed.

A word of warning: It's important not to let curiosity get the best of you. You've probably heard "curiosity killed the cat"; in other words, if you let your curiosity determine the steps you take towards your goals, it could put you in some situations you're better off avoiding.

You've probably noticed there's a tug and pull throughout this book about finding a balance between being a curious adventurer that ends up at the bottom of an avalanche because they didn't think about all the dangers, or a well-prepared, well-armed, and curious adventurer who lives to tell their story. The trick is to find the balance between the two.

So goal-seeking works best when you know about the risks involved while maintaining a healthy respect for attaining it without losing your excitement and curiosity.

When Sir Isaac Newton wondered about what held the moon in place, he had nothing to lose in trying to find out. It's one thing to be curious to see if you can get electrocuted by sticking your finger in a light socket; it's another to end up on the other side of the room from electrical shock. At that point, the cat would have only eight lives left.

It's important to let curiosity *intelligently* guide even when taking small risks. For example, you might ask someone out on a date and find out they're married. Of course it's not a pleasant feeling, but ultimately it won't ruin your life to have taken that risk. At least you tried, you found out they were inaccessible, you moved on. But your curiosity gave you the courage to try.

Goddard often risked his life for the sake of his curiosity. You don't have to go quite so far as kayaking down the Nile (unless you really want to). But you should keep a healthy sense of curiosity and wonder for the world around you as it will take you places far more interesting than where you are today.

You may not have heard the second part of "curiosity kills the cat": "...but satisfaction brings it back!"

Action: **Meet with a friend, mentor or partner to discuss your life list in detail.**

This lesson is for you to set a date with a friend, mentor or life partner to discuss your life list.

As you talk about each goal, make note of which ones resonate with you and inspire you the most, then star those goals.

Then discuss ways to make your goals safe and achievable without "killing the cat."

Lesson

FEED YOUR MIND

Human beings are preoccupied with feeding their bodies. They labor over the decision about where to go for lunch, then make a grocery list so they don't have to repeat the same dinner twice in a week. Food is top-of-mind in our society: Breakfast, lunch, dinner, eating out, eating in, snacks at home, snacks in the car, snacks in the movie theater, even snacks while running.

Of course it's important to feed our bodies, but we should never stop feeding our minds.

John Goddard stayed mentally sharp throughout his life thanks to the challenges he set for himself. In fact, he had distaste for avoiding mental challenge, and shuddered to think about how much time people wasted in front of the television. He reasoned those 40 hours per week they engaged in mindless activity could be spent fulfilling their dreams, instead of numbing themselves to the events of the day.

If you have a similar habit, it may be time to cut back and invest your time more wisely. Rather than watch a half-hour reality show, you could read a book. Rather than watch television over your lunch break you could do a crossword puzzle, chat with friends, or write a letter. It's easy to make small changes that will lead to feeding your mind more amply than you have in the past.

Sometimes you don't have to sacrifice anything but a little time out of your day (and is it really a sacrifice if it produces something worthwhile?) If you take just 15 minutes to tackle any of the following activities, you'll be feeding your mind and staying sharp:

- Reading: newspapers, books, reputable journals, online magazines, blogs
- Games: crossword puzzles, online chess, Sudoku, Scrabble
- Stimulating conversation: with friends, family, colleagues, peers, the neighborhood grocery, the man at the gas station, an old woman in the park, the lady at the library (talk about feeding your mind!)
- Writing: fiction, non-fiction, blogs, articles, letters to the editor, etc.
- Research: take notes on a variety of subjects, learn about new things, information gathering for your novel
- Hobbies: do-it-yourself projects, astronomy, painting, quilt-making, woodworking

When it boils down to it, there are thousands of activities you can use to quell your boredom and stimulate your mind. Many don't require a heavy investment of time, labor, or money. They just require that you turn off the boob tube and shift your focus.

Give it a try for one week to see how much better you feel. You should never stop learning ... and your mind will thank you!

Action: **Find a book or eBook about one of your goals. Read it or listen to it on audiobook.**

Research one of your goals, and set out to learn as much about it as you can. This exercise is pretty self-explanatory, so we'll continue on to Lesson 40.

Lesson 40

LEARN FROM ROLE MODELS

Every path in front of you goes somewhere, though most don't lead to success. Your role models chose the right path. But knowing the correct path to success isn't always easy. The world is a very big place, and many dreams take more than a day to complete. You may feel that no matter how many steps you take forward towards your goal, you end up that many or more backward. The path becomes even more unclear, and time is ticking away.

To help you cut through your uncertainties, it would help to learn from people who have encountered and conquered the same challenges. Role models have been there and done it well, so learning how they got from point A to point B will be invaluable light to shine on your path towards your goal.

They can be of any age, gender, race, spiritual belief, or cultural background. It's their accomplishments that make them a role model, not their outer trappings (even though some things like cultural and ethnic influences guide the paths they take).

There are many ways to study role models. For example:

Historical: Benjamin Franklin's autobiography gives you access to one of the world's most famous renaissance men. He wrote about his productivity habits, the ways he practiced writing, and explained some of the fundamental decisions that shaped his life.

Contemporary: Many young children look up to athletes. But there is no shortage of successful high-achievers for you to learn from, from famous investors and philanthropists, to entrepreneurs and inventors. Even someone in your home town who has successfully stayed in business when others have closed; or someone who broke out of the mold and accomplished what others said they wouldn't or couldn't.

Personal: This can be someone you have close, personal access to that will allow you to pick their brain to understand why they do things the way they do, and the steps they took to create their success. Quite often, interviewing someone in a personal context can lead them to mentoring you to achieve your goal. Good things often comes in surprising packages!

What you learn from role models can reduce your learning curve and help you get to your goal quicker. Your role models have gone through what you're going through, and they've learned lessons along the way. By taking those lessons to heart, you can avoid obstacles you would otherwise have to overcome.

In essence, their experience is walking ahead of you to kick away the stumbling blocks that can get in your way, and to help avoid deep potholes.

If a role model has learned how to tackle life and achieve success, you can use their knowledge for your benefit. So it's important to set your ego aside and pay attention to their advice or the actions they took. You also need to accept the fact your role models know more than you, because they've already accomplished what you're trying to do.

Don't forget that role models aren't a perfect guide for handling everything in your life. They are human beings with flaws and challenges. So instead of idolizing them, learn from them.

Action: **Go online, read forums, go to a seminar or a Meetup group with like-minded individuals, sign up for a class. Or ask around until you find a role model who has achieved the same goal.**

If you have yet to find a mentor or friend who has achieved the same goal as yours, now is the time to look for that special person. Keep in mind you don't have to agree with everything they say or their approach; this is simply someone to learn from. And you can even learn from their mistakes!

They might not be interested in a long-term relationship, but you can glean useful information from emails or brief conversations. Ask them to talk to you, even if only for an informational interview via Skype or email, or over a quick cup of coffee.

Attend lectures, read forums, network with associates and people in your industry. Find ways to interact with someone who knows more than you do about your area of interest.

Lesson 41

MASTERING COMMUNICATION

John Goddard considered language so important that he included "Learn French, Spanish, and Arabic" on his life list. He knew that learning to speak one or more languages would be a vital part of experiencing the richness of the life and culture around him.

No matter how busy life got, no matter how many responsibilities there were, to Goddard there was no excuse not to learn another language. He was an avid writer who published a book about his adventures in Egypt – fulfilling one of his life goals – and recognized the importance of communication from a very early age.

He also knew that mastering communication would have positive results that would echo throughout many areas of his life, from being able to hold better conversations to sharing adventures with his readers. Goddard was a lecturer who spent some 200 days a year giving speeches about his experiences, which would have been difficult without some mastery of different languages as he spoke to people in a variety of cultures.

Learning other languages has many positive effects. You not only gain access to an entirely different culture, you learn about that culture in ways you couldn't if you weren't multilingual. For instance, many people who study ancient texts prefer to study the original mother tongue to have a better grasp on what they're studying.

It's hard to go through life without a thorough concept of words and the power they have to captivate an audience, interest a reader, or relate to someone personally. Which is why you shouldn't ignore the power of learning different languages and ways to communicate.

Action: **Make a commitment to improve your command of language, and become a better communicator.**

If you don't know another language, you may want to add this to your life list. However, if you have no desire to learn a second language (or have already mastered one), you might consider any of the following to improve your communication skills:

- Sign up for a word-of-the-day service that will expand your vocabulary.

- Practice writing one eloquent sentence a day which will improve your language skills bit by bit.

- Enroll in a creative writing or basic English course, depending on how much assistance you need to improve your command of language.

- Join a Toastmasters club or equivalent if public speaking still trips you up.

- Learn the jargon associated with one of your goals.

Wherever you go, whomever you're with, you need to be an effective communicator as you'll need to vocalize or write your needs while attaining your goals.

Lesson 42

RECONNECTING WITH YOUR SPIRITUALITY

It's difficult to explore the world as much as John Goddard did and not feel some sort of connection with nature. But for him, the connection went much deeper than simply admiring a sunset in a strange land; to him, exploration came with a certain spiritual strength.

Goddard once spent months in Africa in an area that hadn't seen human beings in thousands of years. Spending most of the time by himself, he said that in opening his mind, body, and spirit to the influences of nature he found a different sort of strength that did away with depression and stress. He said, "That's where I found God."

In your own life it's possible to connect with a deeper source of love and happiness, but you have to know where to look. Goddard said he focused on mind, body, and spirit goals each day. Many people only think about mind or body goals, forgetting there is an extra dimension to life that can't – and shouldn't – be ignored.

What does it mean to work on spiritual goals on a regular basis? Daily life is planted firmly in routine and can be very inflexible. So it can be difficult to connect with the deeper part of yourself when you're thinking about paying bills, getting the kids to bed on time, and trying to figure out what to eat for dinner.

The key to incorporating more spirituality into your life is not to add to what you already do, but rather to eliminate unnecessary things to make more time for contemplation. If you spend time on an iPhone or iPad playing games or texting, you're substituting the spiritual aspects of life with mind-numbing diversions. But when you use the two hours you planned to spend in front of the television and instead go on a hike to commune with nature and a higher power, you've removed the distraction.

It's when we struggle to keep up with the Joneses and worry about what kind of stuff we should buy, or cram as much as possible into a day just because we can, that we disconnect from the more spiritual side of life.

Returning to spirituality doesn't have to be as hard as you think. If you can find time to get out into nature and reflect on what your purpose in life is, you'll begin to live a life of higher consciousness. It sure as heck beats living on autopilot.

So what in your life can you eliminate to connect with nature and the source of all life? What can you do to become closer with the ethereal core of your being to bring you back in touch with who you are as a human being?

Action: **Remove a distraction or commitment from your life to make time to reconnect with your spirituality.**

Choose something to eliminate from your schedule so you can allow your spiritual side to emerge (or re-emerge).

Some examples of ways to unplug and reconnect are:

- Go for walks or runs instead of going to a group fitness class.

- Turn off the radio or audiobooks during your commute, and just be in the quiet.

- Unplug from the television.

- Refuse to surf the Web.

- Turn off personal emails, Facebook and all social media.

- Leave work a half hour early, and use that time for reflection.
- Arrive home ten minutes early each night, and spend that time in quiet contemplation before you enter the house.
- Pray, meditate or journal your thoughts about your spirituality.

Only you know what you can remove from your life to open space for the Divine.

Lesson 43

ESCAPE THE HERD

The "herd mentality" was discussed earlier because human beings have a strong need to be part of something which isn't necessarily a bad thing, because being part of a group can come with plenty of advantages. For example, the explosion of social media's popularity could be described as an inherent "herding instinct."

But in modern society being part of the "herd" usually happens when someone lacks the independence to form their own identity.

For many people being part of the herd means living the life society programmed for them: Go to grade school, go to high school, go to college, get a job, raise a family, watch the family grow up, and retire. However, when things become rote, predictable, stale and stagnant – and life is devoid of rich experiences – then there's a problem with the herd mentality.

Placing so much emphasis on being part of a herd stifles creativity and identity. When you derive your identity from the herd, you tend to focus on superficial ways of measuring yourself. You believe your job and the acquisition of status symbols such as a sports car or a fancy house measure your success, when in reality they have very little to do (if at all) with who you are as a person.

But what if you're interested in a life that's richer than going to work and watching television all night? What if you feel you aren't challenged by your cookie-cutter lifestyle (if you're living one)? And that you need more stimulation if you're going to forge your own identity?

To escape the herd you need to stop viewing yourself in terms of what you own, and start viewing yourself in terms of the actions you take. Yes, your profession defines you somewhat, but a job is what you do and not who you are.

What do you do in your free time? Do you learn more about the world around you? Where do you challenge yourself? What skills do you possess that separates you from the herd? Are you more concerned about the quality of the life you'll live, or the quality of the things around you? Do you have a life list or a wish list?

Once you set goals that will make you happy and become the standard for how you should be living, you won't fear leaving the herd to venture out on your own. Doing so will build more confidence, happiness, and long-term fulfillment from now and into the future.

And don't forget, you'll be able to share all your adventures with the herd when you get back home. Or at least send them a postcard. But you won't be sitting in front of the television wishing you had a life – you'll be living it!

Action: **Get away from it all, and write down ideas that pop into your head.**

Try hard to take a day off work or get away from the family for one full day (this is why there are sick leave or vacation days). Gently explain to your family that you need a little time to think, to smooth your feathers, and to come up with some fun ideas for adventures.

During this time away you can...

- Exercise by yourself.
- Journal by yourself.

- Perform activities that allow your mind to wander, and give you time to ponder your goals and relax without interruptions.

Take time to evaluate where you are at this point in time, and imagine possibilities for your life ahead.

Lesson 44

IT'S ABOUT TIME!

Is there a resource more precious than time? To John Goddard, the emphatic answer was no.

Time is the most precious commodity you have, so it's important to make the best use of it. It's not difficult to do all the things he did (111 out of his original 127 goals) if you have thousands of years in which to do them. But Goddard managed them in a single lifetime because he knew there was no excuse to procrastinate. Life is too short and he was very well aware of it.

What is procrastination, if not a denial about the time we have on earth before our time runs out? By continuing to tell ourselves we have tomorrow, and then another and another, we're borrowing against our future. And trust me, that's one loan you can't pay back.

The attitude of "it's about time" means placing emphasis on the here and now. What are you doing today to reach your dreams? What are you building today that will still be standing years from now?

Promises of future action might satiate our need to feel like we're making progress, but in reality they do nothing to help us achieve our goals. When a week goes by, and then a month and then a year, we realize our rationalizations only serve to avoid the work it takes to achieve success. We become the fools rushing in where the angels indeed feared to tread, especially since they're off having adventures around the world!

How many times have you seen an accident on the news, and thought about the victim and how they thought they had years to live? No one can predict when they'll leave this earth, and it's a sad fact our time here is temporary. But in a way, it can have a liberating effect on the way you approach your dreams.

Start living your life with the following philosophy in mind: That today and every day going forward you are going to accomplish what you wished you had accomplished yesterday. When you come to the end of your life the memory of pain, stress, and fear will no longer exist. It's only the accomplishments you create during your lifetime that will stay behind.

If you want to build an amazing life, you can't do it sitting on a lawn chair sipping lemonade, or watching another reality show (the concept of that is interesting since they're living the reality and you're not). You're eventually going to have to create a foundation for your goals (your life list), pick up bricks (your actions), and get stacking (your adventures!).

Don't you think it's about time you got started?

Action: **Take action by using your personal calendar to schedule meaningful commitments.**

Review your life list and ask yourself what you feel good about having accomplished, and what you feel you've let slide.

Now ask yourself what you could do to better use your time pursuing things that matter to you.

This exercise is for you to use your calendar to take action. What do you hope to accomplish or experience in the next month? Schedule your days as best you can by arranging meaningful commitments you'll be proud of at the end of one month.

(Scheduling can mean many things, including spending time with your mentor/role model, time for research, time for yourself to regroup, going to seminars, groups, or walking in the park. Just as long as it's productive and part of your goal intention, schedule whatever you can to help you get closer to your goals.)

Lesson 45

DON'T BE SO PRACTICAL

People who are practical are often problem-solvers. They save money for the future and are thrifty, straight-minded, well-balanced, and live a life of relative comfort.

But trying to carry on a conversation with them can sometimes be boring, dull and uninteresting because they've "practicaled" themselves into a mundane existence. Oh-hum.

Yes, it's good to be practical, but not so practical you lose all sense of risk and wonder. It wasn't very practical of Goddard to explore the areas he ventured into. He put himself in many dangerous situations that could have conceivably gone worse than they did. He learned how to step out of the box of practicality, and found a balance between impracticality and putting his life in danger.

Many people throughout history are remembered for when they chose to be impractical. Christopher Columbus, for example, couldn't by all rights be considered a very practical explorer. He was incorrect about the size of the earth (meaning, if North and South America had stood between him and Asia, he might not have survived his first voyage across the Atlantic Ocean).

Being impractical doesn't mean you have to be so bold that your actions border on foolhardy. Lesson 13 mentioned that Gen. George Patton never took counsel of his fears. Essentially, that same lesson bears out here: Don't use fear as an excuse when it's the only thing standing in your way.

Being impractical therefore means you should take calculated risks, and if you really want to attain your goals you'll have no problem risking failure. You've probably tripped and fallen, or stumbled going up stairs. Yet, you don't let those types of failures get in the way of the fact you need to walk to get places.

Well, you need to walk through your life to get places, which requires putting yourself out there, becoming a little vulnerable, asking daring questions, and making bold decisions.

It might be a practical decision not to ask someone to marry you because you might get turned down. But if you love someone, ultimately you need to risk asking them to marry you. Otherwise, you'll spend the rest of your life wondering what their answer would have been. It's the same in life: Ultimately, practicality needs to step aside to allow risk-taking to help you achieve your goals.

So don't be so practical! Get a little foolish from time to time. You might be surprised to see what happens when you let your hair down a bit.

Action: **Do something impractical that gets you closer to your goal.**

This exercise is about doing something that feels so radical and out of your comfort zone that it could be a little embarrassing for you to share with friends or family. You need to enjoy the thrill of doing something even if you think it's nonsensical, silly or, well, impractical!

The first step is to make a significant investment in pursuing your goals. Choose a way to invest in your goal that requires one of the following:

- A financial investment
- A time investment
- An energetic investment

Some "impractical" but exciting examples of this are:

- Take a weekend to do nothing but work on that novel you've been outlining.

- Spend an entire day taking kayaking lessons.

- Sell some stocks and invest the money in inventory for your budding business.

- Hire a marketing firm to spread the word about your charity, business, or social change movement.

- Paint or sculpt your biggest piece yet.

- Find a group of musicians to record a demo with you.

Identify an impractical investment that excites you, and then start investing in yourself!

Lesson 46

VALUING YOUR TIME

In Lesson 44 we talked about the importance of time. But now we're going to discuss time management in a way that's a little more comprehensive.

"Valuing your time" means knowing that every day you have a 24-hour budget to work with. As was mentioned before, everyone has the same amount of time in a day, which means if you're going to get ahead in life you're going to have to budget your time more wisely. And here are a few ways to go about that:

- **Protect your productive time:** Did you know a brief distraction can linger a long time even after the distraction goes away? That's the negative impact that one knock on your office door can have. So get a little ruthless with your productivity time, and let people know you want no distractions unless there's an emergency. Post a sign outside your door and lock it if they don't get the hint. Have incoming calls go straight to your answering machine (and if you have a land line phone and/or cell phone turn off the ringer).

- **Eliminate time wasters:** If your method of handling job stress is to crash in front of your television two hours every night, you need some different stress-reducing strategies. Remember, when you're on your deathbed you won't find yourself saying, "I wish I had watched more TV."

- **Value the time of others:** It sends a strong message of respect if you show others that you value their time just as much as your own. Communicate this to them briefly and gently in emails, meetings, or during phone conversations. Don't say, "You're wasting my time." Say instead, "I don't want to waste your time."

- **Have new experiences:** Your time is valuable even if you have a daily routine. But sometimes your time is best spent having fun, exciting experiences. When you reflect back on your life you'll most likely remember an experience and not the day of the week it happened. So try new things and meet new people.

Consider time as a valuable asset, and you should get a return on your investment. Start doing things that might not always be the most comfortable way to spend your time but can result in the most amount of satisfaction.

When you realize how valuable your time truly is, you'll begin to see why you should make it a huge priority.

Action: **Evaluate your time usage.**

Look into time usage strategies such as the Pomodoro technique (a time management process developed by Francesco Cirillo in the late 1980s that uses a timer to break down work into intervals).

Commit to carving out time in a way that maximizes your personal preferences.

Discover what strategies enable you to maximize your time usage. Do you need to hang out at a coffee shop to write on your laptop, or stay late after work to be most productive? Are you a morning person or a night owl?

Are you most productive if you tackle tasks in chunks, allowing yourself to take breaks after specific increments of time? Or do you perform best if you devote entire days to projects?

Analyze how you're currently managing your time (or if you aren't), then devise a schedule to utilize your time better to your advantage.

Lesson 47

KEEP ADDING TO YOUR LIFE LIST

The oddity of John Goddard's life list is that he wrote it when he was just 15 years of age. But what really made the list unique is that he kept promises to himself by taking action, and kept adding to the list when potential experiences excited him.

This doesn't mean he replaced old goals with new ones. One of his goals was to fly to the moon – one that ultimately went unfulfilled but stayed on the list because it still appealed to him.

Your life list is about what appeals to you, so keep adding to it as the years go on. After all, it's new experiences that challenge and invigorate you. If you keep only to your original list, you may find after a few years your goals have changed.

Keeping everything you come up with on your list can be used as a record of your interests, how they change (and how you change), and what you ultimately achieve. It becomes a litmus test of how you challenge yourself and how much you succeed.

A regular re-evaluation of your priorities will help "adjust your rudder" as you sail through life. You'll see if you're getting off course by focusing on goals rather than adjusting them to match what makes you truly the happiest and most fulfilled. Additionally, if you've been following the lessons in this book you'll begin to check goals off of your list just as Goddard did.

What if you achieve all your goals much quicker than you thought you would? Would your life be over? Heck no! You'll keep adding new challenges to kick the list up a notch or more.

Your life goals aren't truly adventures without the experience of something new. The goal of publishing a book, for example, is only new if you haven't published one before. But what happens when you get published (i.e., an eBook)? Maybe your next new goal could be to write a novel that could make it on the *New York Times* bestseller list.

If you keep improving yourself, keep challenging yourself, and keep aligning your goals with your happiness, you're sure to get the most out of your life list just as John Goddard did.

Action: **Evaluate your life list and add at least three things to it.**

As you pursue your dreams you'll want to add new goals and experiences to your list. Don't replace the old ones as they are a record of your journey.

This lesson is for you to expand on the goals you've already listed. Add some fun, purposeful and outrageous new adventures and experiences to your life list. Dream a little; live a lot!

Lesson 48

CHERISH YOUR ACCOMPLISHMENTS

John Goddard was grateful for everything in his life. He was grateful to have been born in the 20th century, an extraordinary time in which he experienced both piloting a jet and exploring the far reaches of the world. He was grateful to have lived a rich family life with his wife and six children. He was grateful to have had the opportunities to achieve his life goals, and share those accomplishments with the many audience members during his lectures.

An "attitude of gratitude" is a wonderful feeling to have (see Lesson 50), because it indicates you're happy and healthy right at this very moment. It's a positive affirmation for your life, and seems to pay dividends in the way you live your life. You'll be more likely to embrace challenges and appreciate the good times while they last if you cherish your accomplishments.

It's not always easy to take on new challenges. When you're facing possible rejection and obstacles, it can be worthwhile to take a look back on what you've achieved and say, "I feel good about how far I've come, even if I want to travel farther." It helps remind you what you're capable of, which in turn builds confidence for the challenges ahead.

Long after you leave this earth all that will remain are the accomplishments you left behind. We marvel at the Egyptian pyramids because they're a reminder of the magnificent technology that enabled the pyramids to be built. The aqueducts the Romans built are still standing today.

Your accomplishments will ultimately constitute your legacy, so be proud of them! If you don't feel a lot to be grateful for at the moment, then make new goals and cherish what you've accomplished thus far. There will always be something for you to be happy about, even if it's only having the strength to make it this far in your life. With life's many challenges, that is indeed quite an accomplishment.

It's important not to become arrogant about your accomplishments, but to cherish them with a healthy dose of humility. Be thankful for them and bless them in your own private time, and don't spend time bragging about them to others.

Gratitude comes with its own intrinsic rewards. When you separate yourself from people's opinions – both complaints and praises – you realize the results of all your hard work is your reward.

Action: **Make a list of the things you've already accomplished.**

Even though you're pursuing some pretty lofty goals, you've also accomplished many things over the course of your life. Be sure to acknowledge your accomplishments, and celebrate your experiences and past achievements by writing them down on a list.

This exercise is to include small personal victories that are only important to you, and hold a private celebration in which you honor yourself.

Maybe you could make a special meal, toast yourself with a glass of wine, watch your favorite movie, or take yourself out to eat somewhere that's very special to you. You might want to light candles or put on special music to enhance your celebration.

Celebrate your accomplishments in a personal, private way. Then keep your list tucked somewhere safe as it's your legacy!

Lesson 49

INVEST IN YOURSELF

How do you know if you're investing in yourself? As they say "the proof is in the pudding." When you make an investment in something, you do it with the hope and faith the investment will grow. Similarly, when you go for a run you're investing in the time and effort it takes to improve your fitness.

But if you don't take time for a run, then where's your investment? It's wherever your attention switches to: Commuting to work, watching a television show, or reading the newspaper.

There's a huge difference between passing time and spending time. If you're going to reach your goals, you're going to need to start investing time on yourself. Think of all of the possible investments you can make:

- Fitness: Go to the gym, run, lift weights, swim, cycle, hike, etc.

- Reading/writing: Brush up on your writing skills, learn the difference between fiction and non-fiction, blog, research, write your novel or screenplay.

- Work (personal or business): Spend extra time making something exist that didn't exist before, whether it's cleaning gutters, building a dollhouse for your daughter, landscaping a garden, making a presentation to your company's board, or developing an idea for a new product.

There are limitless ways in which you can invest time in yourself, but they can come at some sort of price, whether it's time, energy, money or even comfort. When you go for a run, you sacrifice time and comfort for your long-term benefit. When you build a dollhouse you sacrifice time with family on the weekends and cost for the materials. But the initial investments are well worth the final results.

Avoiding time-wasters that result in short-term pleasure will help cultivate a habit of investing in your long-term future. That's what John Goddard did, and he didn't regret anything for one single moment.

Action: **Choose one self-indulgent investment of time.**

This exercise is about investing in yourself by doing something you truly want to do. You're going to indulge in an activity or pursuit that feeds your soul and makes you glad to be alive.

Ask yourself how much time you're spending doing things people think you should be doing or want you to do. Think through the list of things you want to do for your own pleasure, fulfillment or joy (some of these activities will overlap, but some will be distinctly different). Then take time to engage in something that brings you joy, pleasure or fulfillment.

Lesson 50

AN ATTITUDE OF GRATITUDE

In Lesson 48 on cherishing your accomplishments, we talked about how important it is to have gratitude in your life. A message you could take from Goddard's life might be to make having an attitude of gratitude a habit (what a mouthful!).

Goddard took time every morning to reflect on the tremendous gratitude he had for his life. He was thankful for being healthy, for having a fabulous wife, terrific children and grandchildren, and for his amazing friendships all over the world. So amazing in fact that he could show up in places like Nairobi, Cairo or Mexico City and simply say "I'm here!" and they would welcome him into their homes without hesitation.

Goddard described gratitude as "feeling comfortable as a member of the human family." When you're grateful you feel accepted as a human being, particularly when you're grateful for the family and friendships that ultimately form the happiness in your life.

He made a habit out of feeling grateful and that led to a sense of well-being and fulfillment. Take a proactive attitude toward joy and fulfillment. Don't let it be something you'll achieve some day, but rather something you're doing **today**.

Just as muscular fitness happens by exercising and mental fitness comes through stimulating the mind, your happiness will be an active emotional exercise. And nowhere is that exercise more effective than in developing an attitude of gratitude.

Action: **Make a list of the things you've learned and ways you've grown.**

Start by making a list of five things you have to be thankful for. If you can't conceive of having a life like John Goddard's at this point, you can at least be thankful for something as simple as the sun coming up another day.

Add to it as it jogs your memory about other things or people you may have forgotten to include.

Then choose a goal (or a set of goals that work together) to tackle in the upcoming year.

Establish a new plan based on your successes and what you learned from your setbacks to help you have an even better year next year!

CONCLUSION

What made John Goddard so special, and what set him apart from other adventurers?

In the lessons provided in this book you'll hopefully see that many of his successes – while unique and inspiring – are not unattainable. Sure, you may have different goals than him, but the underlying principles and lessons are universal.

What ultimately made Goddard special was that he lived these principles to such an extent that it provides a beacon to people who are unsure about what to do in their own lives.

Once you finish these lessons you will undoubtedly notice how much you've grown as a person. You now have a clearer picture of what's important to you and how to accomplish goals you previously viewed as wishful thinking. You have become healthier and happier, and have a better grip on the direction you want your life to take.

Just like John Goddard, you too can live a life full of adventure, exploration, and rich relationships. It's not as difficult as you think, but it will require a rewiring of your priorities, your mindset, and some hard work on your part.

What do you do with your time that might need changing? What goals have you written down (hopefully you've done this part; otherwise, what in the heck have you been doing with your time?). What are you thankful for? What adventures have you always wanted to achieve, but have never seemed to get off the ground beyond their initial planning phase?

For Goddard, his intention to succeed began with writing down everything he thought was necessary to live an incredible, adventurous life.

He made them clear and specific, and didn't allow fear to sabotage his excitement.

Writing the list is simple – you just choose the things that will make you feel the happiest. Ultimately achieving your goals comes down to intention and follow-through.

No matter what you want out of life, there is a way you can turn it into a reality. But finding ways to accomplish them isn't simple, or you would have achieved your goals by now. Pursuing your goals will put a number of challenges, fears, and mental blocks in your way. So it's your responsibility to follow through with your plans and grow as a result of the experience.

At the end of the day your life isn't only about goals and achievement; it's also about recognizing the limited time you have on this earth, and asking yourself how you can make the most of it.

When your life comes to a close, what kind of events will you want to reflect on? Will you wish you had spent more time in front of the television or reading the newspaper? Or that you invested in yourself and achieved your goals?

You already know the answer.

Recap of Lessons Learned From John Goddard:

Know what you want.

Dream BIG.

Write it down.

Put your list where you can see it every day.

Set deadlines.

Stop making excuses.

Be ready to overcome obstacles and adversity.

Have no regrets.

For more information about Goddard's life list:
http://www.johngoddard.info/life_list.htm

FREE SMART Goals Worksheet and step-by-step video available for immediate download.

www.Get-Smart-Goals.com

My two sons Carter and Tyler (on each end) and my brother Joel (front) joined me for this picture with John Goddard when he spoke at one of our events in October 2007.

About the Author

Twelve years ago Vic Johnson was totally unknown in the personal development field. Since that time he's created six of the most popular personal development sites on the Internet. One of them, www.AsAManthinketh.net has given away over 400,000 copies of James Allen's classic book. Three of them are listed in the top 5% of websites in the world (English language).

This success came despite the fact that he and his family were evicted from their home 16 years ago and the next year his last automobile was repossessed. His story of redemption and victory has inspired thousands around the world as he has taught the powerful principles that created incredible wealth in his life and for many others.

Today he serves more than 300,000 subscribers from virtually every country in the world. He's become an internationally known expert in goal-achieving, and has hosted his own TV show, *Goals 2 Go*, on TSTN.

His book, *13 Secrets of World Class Achievers,* is the number one goal-setting book at both the Kindle store and Apple iBookstore.

Another best seller, *Day by Day with James Allen,* has sold more than 75,000 copies and has been translated into Japanese, Czech, Slovak and Farsi.

Vic's three-day weekend seminar event, *Claim Your Power Now,* has attracted such icons as Bob Proctor, Jim Rohn, Denis Waitley and many others.

His websites include:

AsAManThinketh.net

Goals2Go.com

GettingRichWitheBooks.com

TheChampionsClub.org

MyDailyInsights.com

VicJohnson.com

ClaimYourPowerNow.com

LaurenzanaPress.com

DiabeticKitchen.com

Other Books by Vic Johnson

52 Mondays: The One Year Path To Outrageous Success & Lifelong Happiness

The Magic of Believing: Believe in Yourself and The Universe Is Forced to Believe In You

How To Write A Book This Weekend, Even If You Flunked English Like I Did

Day by Day with James Allen

Goal Setting: 13 Secrets of World Class Achievers

It's Never Too Late And You're Never Too Old : 50 People Who Found Success After 50

Self Help Books: The 101 Best Personal Development

How I Created a Six Figure Income Giving Away a Dead Guy's Book

Think and Grow Rich: The Lost Secret

How To Make Extra Money: 100 Perfect Businesses for Part-Time and Retirement Income

www.ingramcontent.com/pod-product-compliance
Lightning Source LLC
Chambersburg PA
CBHW070448050426
42451CB00015B/3394